The Blueprint

of

Legal Writing

(Law in Pieces)

Anjanette G. Seymour, LL.M., LL.B. (Hons.)

This work is published as part of the Law in Pieces series of study snippets. It is intended solely for educational purposes and should not be construed as a comprehensive textbook, treatise, or novel. Nothing in this volume constitutes legal advice, nor does it create an attorney–client relationship. Readers should consult qualified counsel and authoritative sources (including statutes, rules, and case law) for guidance on any specific matter.

This book uses fictional case names, citations, parties, quotations, and fact patterns solely for illustrative and instructional purposes. None of the cases or quotations in this book are real, and they should not be treated as authority. Any resemblance to actual persons, entities, cases, or events is purely coincidental. Citations, statutes, and court rules are provided as examples only; readers should independently verify current law, citation requirements, and jurisdiction-specific rules before relying on any authority.

Cover design: Anjanette G. Seymour

ISBN: 9798995892359

TABLE OF CONTENTS

DEDICATION

To every aspiring legal writer who has ever whispered, "I hope I can do this."
May these pages meet you where you are—and walk with you as you learn.
May you write with courage, revise with compassion, and return to the work until your voice sounds like your own.
You belong in this craft.
This book is for you.

INTRODUCTION

"You are allowed to learn. You are allowed to grow. You are allowed to begin again."

Legal writing can feel intimidating, even for the brightest minds. Not because you lack ability, but because you may just need a bit more practice.

This book is rooted in kindness and the belief that every legal writer deserves guidance that feels human.

You will not find judgment here. You will not find assumptions about what you "should" already know.

Instead, you will find:

- **gentle structure**
- **clear models**
- **step-by-step breakdowns**
- **simple explanations of complex ideas**
- **encouragement woven into every chapter**

This book is built for the student who wants to understand, not just perform. For the new lawyer who wants to feel confident, not exposed. For the returning professional who wants to rebuild their foundation without shame. For the independent learner who wants a guide that feels like a steady hand, not a spotlight.

Legal writing is not a test of worthiness. It is a craft — one you can learn, strengthen, and master piece by piece.

As you move through these pages, I hope you feel supported. I hope you feel capable. I hope you feel seen.

Most of all, I hope you discover that your voice — your clear, confident, disciplined legal voice — has been waiting for you all along.

Let's begin gently. Let's build steadily. Let's learn without fear.

CHAPTER ONE

What Legal Writing *Is* — And What It Is Not

Legal writing is not a talent. It is not a gift. It is not a secret language whispered in the hallways of elite institutions.

Legal writing is a **discipline** — a craft built from structure, clarity, and purpose. It is learned, practiced, refined, and strengthened over time.

1. Legal Writing Is a Tool of Power, Not Performance

In law school, legal writing is often treated as a performance — a test of who "gets it" and who doesn't. In practice, however, legal writing is a **tool of power**. It is how lawyers:

- persuade judges
- inform clients
- advise partners
- communicate with agencies
- shape outcomes

Legal writing is not about sounding smart. It is about **being understood**.

A judge does not reward flourish. A partner does not reward theatrics. A client does not reward complexity.

They reward clarity.

2. Legal Writing Has a Purpose: To Guide the Reader

Every legal document has a reader with a job to do:

- A judge must decide.
- A partner must evaluate.

- A client must understand.
- An opposing counsel must respond.

Your writing exists to **guide** that reader through the law, the facts, and the conclusion you want them to reach.

This means legal writing is:

- **Structured** — because readers rely on predictable organization
- **Precise** — because ambiguity creates risk
- **Neutral in tone** — because credibility is currency
- **Focused** — because the law rewards relevance

Legal writing is not creative writing, though it requires creativity. It is not academic writing, though it requires analysis. It is not storytelling, though it requires narrative skill.

It is its own discipline — and the purpose of this book is that you will understand it piece by piece.

3. The Law Governs the Format — Not the Writer

One of the most misunderstood truths in legal writing is this:

Statutes, rules, and local court requirements govern the format of legal documents.

Not professors. Not partners. Not tradition. Not preference.

This book will teach you:

- how federal rules shape the structure of motions
- how appellate rules dictate the order of brief sections
- how local rules control margins, fonts, spacing, and captions
- how jurisdiction determines citation format

- how statutes and procedural rules determine what must be included

Legal writing is not guesswork. It is compliance.

Once you understand the rules, the structure becomes predictable — even comforting.

4. Legal Writing Is Built From Pieces

Every legal document — from a memo to a motion to a brief — is constructed from **pieces**:

- the caption
- the introduction
- the statement of facts
- the standard of review
- the argument
- the conclusion
- the signature block
- the certificate of service

Each piece has a purpose. Each piece has a logic. Each piece has a required format.

This book will show you how each piece fits into the whole — like an architect explaining the beams, joints, and supports of a structure.

You will learn not only *what* to write, but *why* each part exists.

5. Legal Writing Is a Skill You Build

Many students and new lawyers believe that legal writing is a test — a measure of whether they belong. Legal writing is a **skill**, and skills are built through:

- repetition
- feedback
- revision
- clarity
- structure
- practice

This book is designed to be your companion through that process. A guide to which you can return. A reference you can trust.

6. What This Book Will Teach You

By the time you finish this handbook, you will know:

- how to structure legal documents
- how statutes and rules govern formatting
- how to write clear, credible, persuasive analysis
- how to use block quotes, brackets, ellipses, and redactions correctly
- how to cite cases, statutes, and regulations — with full breakdowns
- how to research using accessible tools
- how to brief a case for a supervising attorney
- how to deliver work that partners trust
- how to edit your writing with professional precision

This book is not just for students. It is for the associate who never received training. It is for the professional returning to practice. It is for the person who was told they were "behind" when they were simply **untaught**.

7. Your Promise to Yourself

Before you move to Chapter Two, make this quiet promise:

"I am allowed to learn. I am allowed to grow. I am allowed to master this."

Legal writing is not a gatekeeping tool. It is a craft. And you are about to become a craftsperson.

CHAPTER TWO

The Architecture of Legal Documents

How Statutes, Rules & Jurisdictions Shape Every Line You Write

Before you ever write a sentence, the law has already drawn the blueprint.

Every motion, every brief, every memorandum, every filing — they all follow structures dictated not by preference, but by **statutes**, **court rules**, and **local requirements**. Understanding this truth is one of the most liberating moments in a legal writer's journey.

You are not guessing. You are not improvising. You are not reinventing the wheel.

You are following a **governed architecture** — a structure designed to ensure fairness, clarity, and consistency across the legal system.

This chapter teaches you how to see that architecture.

1. The Law Governs the Form — Not the Writer

Every jurisdiction has rules that dictate:

- margins
- spacing
- fonts
- caption format
- required sections
- page limits
- signature blocks
- certificates of service

- appendix requirements
- table of authorities
- even how exhibits must be labeled

These rules come from:

- **Federal Rules of Civil Procedure (FRCP)**
- **Federal Rules of Appellate Procedure (FRAP)**
- **State procedural rules**
- **Local court rules**
- **Standing orders of individual judges**
- **Statutes governing specific filings**

Legal writing is not a blank page. It is a **regulated canvas**.

Once you understand the rules, the structure becomes predictable — and predictability is power.

2. Why Courts Require Structure

Courts require uniformity for three reasons:

A. Efficiency

Judges read thousands of pages a month. Uniform structure allows them to find information quickly.

B. Fairness

If every lawyer used a different format, the system would be chaotic. Rules ensure equal footing.

C. Clarity

A predictable structure helps the court understand the argument without distraction.

Legal writing is not about creativity first — it is about **function**.

3. The Universal Building Blocks of Legal Documents

Although jurisdictions differ, most legal documents share core components. Think of these as the **load-bearing walls** of legal writing:

- **Caption**
- **Title of the document**
- **Introduction or preliminary statement**
- **Statement of facts**
- **Standard of review**
- **Argument**
- **Conclusion**
- **Signature block**
- **Certificate of service**

Each of these will be dissected in later chapters, but here we establish the architectural logic behind them.

4. Federal vs. State vs. Local Rules: Why They Matter

Federal Rules

These govern structure in federal courts. They dictate:

- motion requirements
- timing
- formatting
- appendices

- citation rules and format required by the court (and any jurisdiction-specific citation conventions)

State Rules

Every state has its own procedural code. Some mirror federal rules; others differ dramatically.

Local Rules

These are often overlooked — and yet, they are also important.

Local rules may dictate:

- font size
- line spacing
- caption layout
- page numbering
- exhibit labeling
- electronic filing requirements

Judge-Specific Rules

Some judges issue **standing orders** that override local rules.

A well-trained legal writer always checks:

1. Federal or state rules
2. Local rules
3. Judge's standing orders

In that order.

5. Why Format Is Not Optional

Format is not decoration. Format is compliance.

Courts may:

- reject filings
- strike documents
- refuse to consider arguments
- impose sanctions

…if the document violates formatting rules.

This is why legal writing must be taught like architecture — with precision, structure, and respect for the governing code.

6. The Logic Behind Each Required Section

This chapter introduces the *why* behind each part of a legal document. Later chapters will show you *how* to write them.

A. Caption

Identifies the case, parties, court, and document. It is the "address" of the filing.

B. Introduction

Gives the judge a roadmap. Judges often read this first and last.

C. Statement of Facts

Provides the factual landscape. Must be neutral, accurate, and complete.

D. Standard of Review

Tells the court how to evaluate the issue. This frames the entire argument.

E. Argument

The heart of the document. Built from rules, reasoning, and application.

F. Conclusion

States the relief requested — clearly and directly.

G. Signature Block

Your professional seal.

H. Certificate of Service

Proof that all parties received the document.

Each part exists because the law requires it — not because a professor or partner prefers it.

7. The Writer's Mindset: You Are Building, Not Guessing

When you understand that legal writing is architectural, everything changes.

You stop fearing the blank page. You stop wondering what goes where. You stop feeling "behind."

Instead, you begin to see:

- structure
- purpose
- logic
- predictability

You become the architect of your own clarity.

CHAPTER THREE

The Core Structures of Legal Analysis

IRAC, CREAC, CRuPAC, and the Frameworks That Shape Legal Thought

Legal writing is not built on instinct. It is built on **frameworks** — predictable, repeatable structures that guide the reader through your reasoning. These frameworks are the skeleton of legal analysis. They hold the argument upright, give it shape, and ensure that every piece connects logically to the next.

This chapter teaches you the most widely used structures in legal writing: **IRAC, CREAC, and CRuPAC.**

Once you understand these, you can write anything — a memo, a motion, a brief, a case analysis, or a partner-ready research summary.

1. Why Legal Writing Uses Structured Frameworks

Judges, partners, and supervising attorneys read quickly. They skim. They jump to headings. They look for the rule. They look for the application. They look for the conclusion.

Frameworks exist to help them find what they need.

Legal writing is not about surprising the reader. It is about **guiding** them.

A good structure:

- reduces cognitive load
- increases clarity
- builds credibility
- prevents rambling
- ensures logical flow

Think of these frameworks as the **architectural plans** for your analysis. You will fill them with content, but the structure itself is non-negotiable.

2. IRAC — The Classic Framework

IRAC stands for:

- **Issue**
- **Rule**
- **Application**
- **Conclusion**

It is the simplest and most widely taught structure.

I — Issue

A clear, concise statement of the legal question.

Example: "Did the defendant owe a duty of care to the plaintiff under state negligence law?"

R — Rule

The governing law: statutes, cases, regulations.

A — Application

Where you apply the rule to the facts. This is the heart of the analysis.

C — Conclusion

A direct answer to the issue.

IRAC is clean, predictable, and effective — especially for short analyses.

3. CREAC — The Modern, More Persuasive Structure

CREAC stands for:

- **Conclusion**
- **Rule**
- **Explanation**
- **Application**
- **Conclusion (again)**

CREAC is used in many law firms and courts because it is more **reader-friendly** and **persuasive**.

C — Conclusion (front-loaded)

You begin with your answer.

R — Rule

State the governing rule.

E — Explanation

Explain the rule using cases, statutes, and reasoning.

A — Application

Apply the rule to your facts.

C — Conclusion (reinforced)

Restate your answer.

CREAC is ideal for:

- motions
- briefs
- persuasive writing
- complex issues

It respects the reader's time by giving them the answer upfront.

4. CRuPAC — The Framework for Complex, Multi-Authority Analysis

CRuPAC stands for:

- **Conclusion**
- **Rule: Umbrella Rule** (e.g., negligence is the failure to exercise reasonable care under the circumstances).

  R → Specific Elements: e.g., To establish negligence, the plaintiff must prove duty, breach, causation, and damages.
- **Proof of Rule (Authority)**
- **Application**
- **Conclusion**

It is similar to CREAC but emphasizes **authority** — especially when multiple cases or statutes must be synthesized.

C — Conclusion

State your answer first.

Ru — Rule

State the governing legal principle.

P — Proof of Rule (Authority)

This is where you:

- cite cases
- explain holdings
- compare authorities
- show how courts interpret the rule

This section is the "deep dive" into precedent.

Example (what "Proof of Rule" looks like): Suppose you write, "A party who voluntarily undertakes responsibility for another's safety owes a duty of reasonable care when the plaintiff reasonably relies on the undertaking." In the Proof of Rule section, you then support that sentence by synthesizing authority—for example:

- "Courts impose a duty when the defendant's undertaking increases the risk of harm or when the plaintiff relies on the undertaking." *Johnson v. Metro Co.*, 455 F.3d 112, 118 ([CIRCUIT] Cir. [YEAR]).
- "Reliance is reasonable where the defendant makes a specific assurance of safety and the plaintiff proceeds in response to that assurance." *Sands v. Granite Servs.*, 201 F.3d 900, 907 ([CIRCUIT] Cir. [YEAR]).
- "A general statement of concern is not enough; the undertaking must be specific enough to invite reliance." *Lee v. Parkside Props.*, 88 F. Supp. 3d 210, 215 ([DISTRICT] [YEAR]).

A — Application

Apply the synthesized rule to your facts.

C — Conclusion

Restate your answer.

CRuPAC is ideal for:

- appellate briefs
- complex motions
- issues with conflicting authority
- research memos for supervising attorneys

5. How to Choose the Right Framework

Use IRAC when:

- the issue is simple
- the analysis is short
- you are writing for a class or exam

Use CREAC when:

- you are writing a motion or brief
- you want to persuade
- you want to front-load your conclusion

Use CRuPAC when:

- the issue is complex
- multiple cases must be synthesized
- you are writing for a partner or judge
- the law is unsettled

Choosing the right structure is like choosing the right blueprint. The complexity of the project determines the design.

6. The Secret to Mastery: One Point, One Structure

Each issue gets its own IRAC, CREAC, or CRuPAC.

Never combine multiple issues into one structure. Never bury rules inside application. Never skip the conclusion.

Legal writing is modular. Each issue is a **piece** — and your job is to assemble the pieces clearly.

7. A Visual Comparison

IRAC

I – What is the legal question?

R – What is the rule?

A – How does the rule apply?

C – What is the answer?

CREAC

C – Here is the answer.

R – Here is the rule.

E – Here is how courts interpret it.

A – Here is how it applies.

C – Here is the answer again.

CRuPAC

C – Here is the answer.

Ru – Here is the rule.

P – Here is the authority proving the rule.

A – Here is how it applies.

C – Here is the answer again.

8. Why These Structures Work

They:

- reduce ambiguity
- force logical thinking
- prevent missing steps
- build credibility
- help judges skim
- help partners trust your work

A supervising attorney should be able to:

- read your headings
- skim your rule
- glance at your application
- and understand your conclusion

without confusion.

That is the mark of a trained legal writer.

CHAPTER FOUR

Writing Clearly, Concisely & Professionally

Legal writing is not about sounding impressive. It is about being understood.

The most effective legal writers — judges, seasoned litigators, appellate advocates — share one trait: **clarity**. They write so that the reader never struggles, never wonders what the sentence means.

This chapter teaches you how to write with clarity, conciseness, and professional tone — the three pillars of legal style.

1. Clarity: The First Rule of Legal Writing

Clarity is not optional. It is the foundation of credibility.

A judge who cannot understand your writing cannot rule in your favor. A partner who cannot follow your analysis cannot trust your work. A client who cannot grasp your explanation cannot make informed decisions.

Clarity means:

- choosing precise words
- writing direct sentences
- avoiding unnecessary complexity
- guiding the reader through your reasoning

Clarity is not simplicity — it is precision.

The Clarity Test

Ask yourself: **"Can a reader understand this sentence on the first read?"**

If the answer is no, revise.

2. Conciseness: Say Only What Needs to Be Said

Conciseness is not about writing less. It is about writing **exactly enough**.

Legal readers are busy. They skim. They jump to headings. They look for the rule. They look for the application.

Concise writing respects their time.

Conciseness Techniques

- Remove filler ("It is important to note that…").
- Cut throat-clearing ("This memorandum will discuss…").
- Avoid doublets ("null and void," "cease and desist").
- Prefer strong verbs over weak constructions.
- Replace long phrases with short equivalents.

Examples:

- "Due to the fact that" → **"Because"**
- "In the event that" → **"If"**
- "At this point in time" → **"Now"**
- "It is clear that" → **Delete entirely**

Conciseness is clarity's twin.

3. Professional Tone: Neutral, Respectful, Credible

Legal writing is not emotional writing. It is not argumentative in the personal sense. It is not dramatic, sarcastic, or combative.

Professional tone means:

- neutral language

- objective presentation of facts
- respectful treatment of opposing arguments
- confidence without arrogance

Tone is how you build trust.

Professional Tone Examples

Instead of: "The defendant clearly lied." **Write**: "The defendant's testimony conflicts with the documentary evidence."

Instead of: "This argument is ridiculous." **Write**: "This argument lacks support in the record."

Tone is not about politeness — it is about credibility.

4. Sentence Structure: The Architecture of Clarity

Strong legal writing uses strong sentences.

A. Lead with the Actor

Instead of: "It is argued by the plaintiff that…" **Write**: "The plaintiff argues that…"

B. Keep Subjects and Verbs Close

Instead of: "The court, after reviewing the evidence and considering the arguments presented by both parties, held…" **Write**: "After reviewing the evidence and considering both parties' arguments, the court held…"

C. Prefer Active Voice

Active voice is clearer and more direct.

- "The court denied the motion." (active)
- "The motion was denied by the court." (passive)

Passive voice is appropriate when:

- the actor is unknown
- the actor is irrelevant
- the actor should be de-emphasized

Example: “The statute was amended in 2022.”

5. Paragraph Craft: Building Blocks of Analysis

A paragraph is not a collection of sentences. It is a **unit of meaning**.

Each paragraph should contain:

A. A Topic Sentence

This tells the reader what the paragraph is about.

B. Rule or Explanation

If needed, explain the law or concept.

C. Application or Analysis

Show how the rule applies to the facts.

D. A Mini-Conclusion

Wrap up the point.

Paragraphs are the “rooms” of your legal house. Each must have a purpose.

6. Transitions: Guiding the Reader Through the Argument

Transitions are the joints of legal writing. They connect ideas and prevent confusion.

Types of Transitions

- **Logical transitions:** “Therefore,” “However,” “Additionally”
- **Structural transitions:** “First,” “Second,” “Finally”

- **Analytical transitions:** "In contrast," "Similarly," "As a result"

Transitions are not decoration — they are navigation.

7. Avoiding Common Pitfalls

A. Legalese

Avoid archaic or unnecessary terms:

- "Herein," "heretofore," "thereinabove"
- "Said defendant," "aforementioned plaintiff"

Use plain English unless the term has legal significance.

B. Over-quoting

Use quotations sparingly. Explain the rule in your own words.

C. Over-citation

Cite what is necessary — not everything you found.

D. Emotional language

Avoid exaggeration, sarcasm, or personal attacks.

E. Long, winding sentences

If a sentence is more than 25–30 words, check whether it can be split.

8. Tools for Clear, Concise, Professional Writing

A. Read your writing aloud

If you stumble, the reader will too.

B. Use checklists

Later chapters will include editing checklists.

C. Edit in layers

First for structure, then clarity, then conciseness, then tone.

D. Ask: "What does the reader need?"

Legal writing is a service.

CHAPTER FIVE

Paragraph Craft & Transitions

How to Build Analysis That Flows, Connects, and Persuades

Chapter Four focused on sentence-level style: clarity, concision, and tone. This chapter moves up a level. It shows **how paragraphs work together**—how to sequence points, build momentum, and guide the reader through a multi-step argument without losing them.

You will learn how to: (1) make your headings and first sentences form an "outline you can read"; (2) write roadmap sentences that prevent confusion; (3) transition the way legal reasoning actually moves (rule → meaning → application; analogize; distinguish; address counterarguments); and (4) diagnose flow problems quickly during revision.

1. One Paragraph, One Job: Sequencing Your Argument

A common reason briefs feel "choppy" is not sentence quality—it is **sequence**. Each paragraph should do one clear job in the larger structure: state a rule, explain it with authority, apply it to facts, distinguish the other side's cases, or answer a counterargument.

Common paragraph jobs include:

- State the controlling rule (or legal standard).
- Explain/synthesize the rule with authority (why the rule means what you say it means).
- Apply the rule to a specific fact (or set of facts) in the record.
- Analogize or distinguish key authority (show why your case is like—or unlike—the controlling precedent).

A simple sequencing rule: **do the reader's work in the order the reader needs it**. Explain the rule before you apply it. Tell the reader what a case proves before you cite it. And do not drop a conclusion without showing the path.

2. The "Outline You Can Read" Test (Headings + First Sentences)

Quick diagnostic: read only (1) your headings and (2) the first sentence of each paragraph. If that skeleton does not tell a coherent story, the full draft will not either.

Use this 3-step exercise:

- Copy/paste your headings and first sentences into a new page so you can see the argument's skeleton.
- Check whether each sentence logically follows the last (rule → meaning → application → conclusion).
- Fix breaks by reordering paragraphs, rewriting first sentences to state the point, or adding a roadmap sentence before a shift.

3. Roadmaps and Signposts: Keeping the Reader Oriented

When you are about to shift the reader to a new place—new element, new authority, new factual category—use a roadmap sentence. A roadmap is a short promise: "Here is where we are going next, and why."

- Single-issue roadmap: "This section shows that Defendant owed a duty because (1) Defendant undertook responsibility for safety and (2) Plaintiff reasonably relied on that undertaking."
- Multi-factor roadmap: "Courts evaluate foreseeability, control, and public policy; each factor supports imposing a duty here."
- Counterargument roadmap: "Defendant argues reliance was unreasonable; the record shows reliance was reasonable

because Defendant made a specific assurance and Plaintiff had no practical alternative."

4. Transition Moves Lawyers Use (Not Just "However")

Transitions work best when they signal **the reasoning move** you are making—not just a change in tone. Here are transition moves you can reuse:

- **Rule → meaning:** This move explains what the rule *really requires* in plain language—before you start applying it to facts. It answers: "What does this standard mean in practice?" Example: "This standard requires more than general awareness; it requires specific knowledge of the risk."
- **Meaning → application:** This move connects your explanation to the record by showing how the facts satisfy (or fail) the clarified rule. It answers: "Given what the rule means, where do we see that in *these* facts?" Example: "Here, the record shows specific knowledge because Defendant inspected the scaffolding moments before the collapse."
- **Analogize:** "Like the defendant in *Sands*, Defendant made an affirmative assurance and invited reliance."
- **Distinguish:** "Unlike *Sands*, Plaintiff here had no warning signs and no reasonable alternative."
- **Concede-and-pivot:** "Even if the court doubts reliance, the duty still arises because Defendant's conduct increased the risk of harm."

5. Avoiding the "Mega-Paragraph": When to Split and How to Signal

If a paragraph is doing multiple jobs, split it. Common triggers: (1) you introduce a new case; (2) you shift from law to facts; (3) you switch from your argument to the opponent's; or (4) the paragraph runs longer than a half page.

- Add a one-sentence roadmap before the split ("Two cases show why; the first addresses duty, the second addresses reliance.").
- Repeat a key phrase to keep continuity ("This duty arises…" / "This duty also requires…").
- Use a short transition sentence as a hinge ("With the rule established, the remaining question is whether the facts satisfy it.").

6. Quick Flow Checklist (Use During Revision)

- Can you read the headings + first sentences and understand the argument without the rest?
- Does each paragraph do one job (rule, meaning, application, analogy/distinguish, counterargument, remedy)?
- Do you introduce each authority with a purpose ("This case shows…"), before quoting or citing it?
- Before any major shift, did you give a roadmap sentence?
- Did you split "mega-paragraphs" and add hinge sentences ?
- If you can keep these six checks true, your reader will feel guided—even through a complex argument.

CHAPTER SIX

Quotations, Block Quotes, Brackets & Redactions

The Technical Tools That Make Your Writing Precise, Professional & Court-Ready

Legal writing is not only about structure and analysis — it is also about **precision**. Lawyers must quote accurately, modify quotations ethically, and present text in a way that is both readable and compliant with court rules.

This chapter teaches you the mechanics behind:

- short quotations
- block quotations
- brackets
- ellipses
- redactions
- emphasis
- alterations

These tools are the fine instruments of legal writing — the chisels, rulers, and measuring tapes that allow you to work with the law's raw materials.

1. Why Quotation Mechanics Matter

Judges and supervising attorneys expect:

- accuracy
- honesty
- clarity
- professionalism

A misquoted case can damage your credibility. A poorly formatted block quote can frustrate the reader. A missing bracket or ellipsis can change meaning.

Quotation mechanics are not optional — they are part of the architecture of legal writing.

2. Short Quotations

Courts set the line between a short quotation and a block quotation in their rules or style requirements. A common benchmark is **50 words**, but many courts use different limits (often 40 or 60). Always check the governing rules for your court.

How to Format Short Quotations

- Use quotation marks.
- Keep the quote within the paragraph.
- Cite immediately after the quotation.
- Use brackets or ellipses if you modify the text.

Example

The court held that "a duty arises when a party voluntarily undertakes responsibility for another's safety."

Short quotations should be used sparingly. Explain the rule in your own words unless the exact language is legally significant.

3. Block Quotes

Block quotes are used for longer quotations. They are visually distinct, and their formatting is governed by your court's rules and local practice requirements.

When to Use a Block Quote

- When the quotation meets the block-quotation threshold under the governing rules (a common benchmark is 50 words, but local rules vary).
- When quoting statutory language.
- When quoting a key passage from a case.

How to Format a Block Quote

- Start on a new line.
- Indent the entire block (usually 0.5 inches).
- Do **not** use quotation marks.
- Some writers (and some non-brief formats) place the citation on a new line preceded by an em dash for readability, but you should use that style only if it is permitted and consistent with your court's rules and conventions.
- Maintain a blank line before and after the block quote.
- Place the citation after the final punctuation.

Example:

When a quotation exceeds 50 words, it must be set off from the rest of the text. Here is how that "structural room" should look on the page:

The court in *Johnson v. Metro Co.* established the clear criteria for a voluntary undertaking, stating:

> A person who undertakes to render services to another is subject to liability for physical harm resulting from his failure to exercise reasonable care if (a) his failure increases the risk of harm, or (b) the harm is suffered because of the other's reliance on the undertaking. In this scenario, the defendant's preoccupation with other tasks does not excuse the increased

> risk created by a failure to secure the premises, rendering him liable for the plaintiff's injuries. *Johnson v. Metro Co.*, 455 F.3d 112, 118 ([CIRCUIT] Cir. [YEAR]).

Optional style example (citation on a new line):

> A person who undertakes to render services to another is subject to liability for physical harm resulting from his failure to exercise reasonable care if (a) his failure increases the risk of harm, or (b) the harm is suffered because of the other's reliance on the undertaking.
> — *Johnson v. Metro Co.*, 455 F.3d 112, 118 ([CIRCUIT] Cir. [YEAR]).

As this passage illustrates, the defendant's focus on his own duties did not alleviate the duty he had already assumed toward the plaintiff.

4. Brackets: The Tool for Clarity & Accuracy

Brackets allow you to modify a quotation **without altering its meaning**.

Uses of Brackets

A. Adding Clarifying Information

"The defendant [the contractor] failed to secure the scaffolding."

B. Correcting Capitalization

"[T]he court held that…"

C. Inserting Missing Words

"The plaintiff [did not] consent to the search."

D. Replacing Pronouns

"He" → "[the officer]"

Brackets are honesty tools. They show the reader exactly what you changed.

5. Ellipses: Removing Unnecessary Text

Ellipses (…) indicate that you have omitted words from a quotation.

Rules for Ellipses

- Use three dots for omissions within a sentence.
- Use four dots when omitting the end of a sentence (three dots + period).
- Do not distort meaning.
- Do not use ellipses to hide unfavorable language.

  — **Example of what "do not use ellipses to hide unfavorable language" means:**

  Original: "The defendant owed a duty of care; however, the plaintiff's claim fails because she assumed the risk."

  Misleading: "The defendant owed a duty of care …."

  Better: Quote the full sentence or quote the favorable portion **without changing the source's meaning** and then immediately acknowledge the limitation in your own words (with a pin cite).

  Example (quoting the favorable portion, honestly): "The defendant owed a duty of care …." *(pin cite)* But the court ultimately ruled against the plaintiff based on assumption of the risk. *(pin cite)*

Separate example (neutral omission): This example shows an ellipsis used to remove nonessential words without changing the source's meaning.

Original: "The defendant owed a duty of care because he voluntarily undertook responsibility for the plaintiff's safety and assured him the scaffolding was secure."

With ellipsis: "The defendant owed a duty of care because he voluntarily undertook responsibility… and assured him the scaffolding was secure.”

Ellipses are tools of efficiency, not manipulation.

6. Redactions: Protecting Sensitive Information

Redactions are used to remove:

- personal identifiers
- confidential information
- privileged material
- sealed content

Two Types of Redaction

A. Black Bar Redaction

Used in filed documents.

Example: “The witness stated that her address was ████████████.”

B. Bracketed Redaction

Used in quotations.

Example: “The witness stated that her address was [redacted].”

Always follow local rules and protective orders when redacting.

C. How to Redact

In Adobe Acrobat:

- open the PDF
- Go to **Tools → Redact**
- Choose **Apply Redactions** to permanently remove it.

Practice note: You **can correct a redaction, but only before** you apply it. **Once you apply a redaction, the removal is permanent. To correct a redaction <u>before</u> applying it, use one of the following options**:

In Adobe Acrobat (before applying the redaction):

- Select **Edit → Undo** (or press **Ctrl+Z**).
- Right-click the redaction mark and select **Delete**.
- Alternatively, select the redaction mark and press **Delete** on your keyboard.

Practice tip: Run a trial redaction on a mock document before redacting a final filing. Once applied, redactions are permanent.

7. Emphasis: Italics, Bold, and Parentheticals

A. Italics

Used for:

- case names
- emphasis
- foreign words
- defined terms (sparingly)

B. Bold

Rarely used in legal writing. Some courts prohibit it.

C. Parentheticals

Used after citations to explain relevance.

Example: *Smith v. Jones*, 200 F.3d 555, 560 ([CIRCUIT] Cir. [YEAR]) (holding that voluntary undertakings create a duty of care).

Parentheticals are powerful tools of persuasion.

8. Alterations: When You Must Signal a Change

If you change anything in a quotation, you must signal it.

Common Alterations

- **"[cleaned up]"** — used in some jurisdictions to simplify citations (it signals that you removed extra citation clutter like multiple quotation marks, brackets, citations, and parentheticals without changing the meaning).

  Original: "Courts impose a duty when a defendant's undertaking invites reliance." *Johnson v. Metro Co.*, 455 F.3d 112, 118 ([CIRCUIT] Cir. [YEAR]) (quoting *Smith v. Jones*, 200 F.3d 555, 560 ([CIRCUIT] Cir. [YEAR])).

  After: "Courts impose a duty when a defendant's undertaking invites reliance." *Johnson v. Metro Co.*, 455 F.3d 112, 118 ([CIRCUIT] Cir. [YEAR]) **[cleaned up]**

- **"[emphasis added]"** — when you italicize or bold part of a quote (it tells the reader the emphasis was not in the original source).

  Original: "A duty arises when a party voluntarily undertakes responsibility for another's safety." *Johnson v. Metro Co.*, 455 F.3d 112, 118 ([CIRCUIT] Cir. [YEAR]).

  After: "A duty arises when a party *voluntarily undertakes* responsibility for another's safety." *Johnson v. Metro Co.*, 455 F.3d 112, 118 ([CIRCUIT] Cir. [YEAR]) **[emphasis added]**.

- **"[internal quotation marks omitted]"** — when removing nested quotes (it tells the reader the source used quotation marks inside the quotation, and you removed the inner quotation marks for readability).

  Original: "The court explained that a duty exists when the defendant \"assumes responsibility for safety\" and the plaintiff relies on that undertaking." *Johnson v. Metro Co.*, 455

F.3d 112, 118 ([CIRCUIT] Cir. [YEAR]).

After: "The court explained that a duty exists when the defendant assumes responsibility for safety and the plaintiff relies on that undertaking." *Johnson v. Metro Co.*, 455 F.3d 112, 118 ([CIRCUIT] Cir. [YEAR]) **[internal quotation marks omitted]**.

Always check whether your jurisdiction allows these signals.

9. Ethical Quotation Practices

Never:

- change meaning
- omit unfavorable language without acknowledgment
- misquote
- take text out of context
- use ellipses to distort

Your credibility is your currency. Protect it.

10. Putting It All Together: A Model Quotation Section

Here is a fully formatted example combining the tools:

Short-form citation note (*Id.*): *Id.* (italicized) means "the same authority as the immediately preceding citation." Use *Id.* only when the prior citation is to the same source; otherwise, use a different short form or repeat the citation. Use *Id.* at 119 to cite a different page in the same source.

Quick example: Johnson v. Metro Co., 455 F.3d 112, 118 ([CIRCUIT] Cir. [YEAR]). *Id.* at 119.

Example Paragraph

The voluntary-undertaking doctrine imposes a duty when a party "assumes responsibility for another's safety and the other relies on that undertaking." *Johnson v. Metro Co.*, 455 F.3d 112, 118 ([CIRCUIT] Cir. [YEAR]). Courts explain that this duty arises because "the actor's conduct creates a foreseeable risk of harm… and the injured party reasonably relies on the actor's assurances." *Id.* at 119.

Here, the defendant personally inspected the scaffolding, assured the plaintiff it was secure, and instructed him to proceed. The plaintiff relied on these assurances. Therefore, the defendant owed a duty of care.

This is the level of clarity and professionalism your writing will achieve.

CHAPTER SEVEN

Case Citations: Anatomy, Meaning & Jurisdictional Differences

Understanding Every Piece of a Citation — Line by Line, Like an Architect Reading a Blueprint

Legal citations are the coordinates of the law. They tell the reader **where** a case lives, **who** decided it, **when** it was decided, and **how** to find it.

By the end of this chapter, you will be able to:

- read any citation
- understand every component
- identify the court
- identify the reporter
- know whether the case is binding
- know what to italicize in citations (e.g., case names)
- understand jurisdictional differences
- cite cases, statutes, and regulations with confidence

1. Why Citations Matter

Citations are not decoration. They are the **roadmap** to legal authority.

A citation tells the reader:

- where the rule comes from
- who created it
- whether it is binding or persuasive
- how to find the case

- how to verify your argument

A judge cannot rely on your argument unless you show them **where the law lives**.

Citations are the addresses of legal authority.

Note on examples: This chapter uses fictional citations to teach citation anatomy. The examples are not real authority. Readers should always verify authorities and applicable citation rules in their jurisdiction.

2. The Anatomy of a Case Citation (Architectural Breakdown)

Example:

***Rivera v. Harbor Transit Co.*, 248 State Rep. 339, 162 N.E. 99 (1928)**

Now we break it down like an architect labeling each beam, joint, and support.

A. Case Name (italicized)

Rivera ***v. Harbor Transit Co.***

- Always italicized in legal writing.
- "v." means "versus."
- The first name is the plaintiff; the second is the defendant.
- In appellate cases, the names may reflect the parties on appeal.

B. Reporter Volume (not italicized)

248

This is the volume number of the reporter where the case is published.

C. Reporter Abbreviation (not italicized)

State Rep. (example of an official state-reporter abbreviation)

This tells you:

- the jurisdiction (a state court system) (example)
- the reporter series (an official state reporter) (example)
- the court level (which can sometimes be inferred from the reporter and context)

D. First Page of the Case (not italicized)

339

This is where the case begins in the reporter.

E. Parallel Citation (not italicized)

162 N.E. 99

This tells you that:

The Secondary Location. This case is also printed in the North Eastern Reporter (N.E.) at volume 162, page 99.

F. Parenthetical (Court + Year) (not italicized)

(1928)

This tells you:

- the year the case was decided
- sometimes the court (if not clear from the reporter)

If the reporter already identifies the court, only the year is needed.

3. Adding a Pinpoint Citation (Pin Cite)

A **pin cite** tells the reader **exactly where** in the case the quoted or referenced material appears.

Example:

***Rivera v. Harbor Transit Co.*, 248 State Rep. 339, 341 (1928)**

Here:

- 339 = where the case begins
- 341 = the specific page you are referencing

Pin cites are essential for credibility.

4. Federal Case Citations

Federal cases use different reporters.

A. U.S. Supreme Court

Example: ***Adams v. City Board***, 347 U.S. 483 (1954)

Breakdown:

- 347 = volume
- U.S. = United States Reports
- 483 = first page
- (1954) = year

B. Federal Courts of Appeals

Example: ***Smith v. Jones***, 912 F.3d 123 ([CIRCUIT] Cir. [YEAR])

Breakdown:

- F.3d = Federal Reporter, Third Series

[CIRCUIT] Cir. = the [CIRCUIT] Circuit Court of Appeals (example)

C. Federal District Courts

Example: ***Johnson v. Metro Co.***, 455 F. Supp. 3d 112 ([DISTRICT]

[YEAR])

Breakdown:

- [DISTRICT] = the specific federal district court abbreviation (e.g., S.D.N.Y., N.D. Ill.). (example)

Federal citations always tell you the level of the court.

5. State Case Citations (Jurisdictional Differences)

Every state has its own citation system.

A. States Using Regional Reporters

Example ([STATE]): ***People v. Clark***, 202 [STATE] 2d 134 ([YEAR])

Example ([STATE]): ***Smith v. Anderson***, 123 [STATE] App. 4th 456 ([YEAR])

B. States With Their Own Reporters

Example (official state reporter): ***Rivera***, 248 State Rep. 339 (1928)

C. States Using Public Domain Citations

Some states use paragraph numbers instead of page numbers.

Example ([STATE]): ***State v. Brown***, [YEAR]–[STATE]–[CASE NUMBER], ¶ 15

This is why jurisdiction matters — citation formats change.

6. How to Know Whether a Case Is Binding or Persuasive

Citations tell you the **authority level**.

Binding Authority

- **Same jurisdiction**

  What this means: The case comes from the same jurisdiction that will decide your case (for example, the same state or the same federal circuit). Because the same court system created the rule, your judge is generally required to follow it unless it has been overruled or is distinguishable.

- **Higher court**

  What this means: Decisions from higher courts in the same system bind lower courts (e.g., your state supreme court binds your state trial courts; the U.S. Supreme Court binds all courts on federal questions). When a higher court has spoken on the issue, that is usually the starting point for your analysis.

- **Same level court (in some systems)**

  What this means: In some courts, decisions from the same level court can be treated as binding (or strongly persuasive) within that court, depending on local rules and practice. For example, a court may follow its own prior decisions unless there is a reason to depart. Always check jurisdiction-specific rules on horizontal stare decisis.

Persuasive Authority

- **Other jurisdictions**

  What this means: A case from a different jurisdiction (another state, or a different federal circuit) is not binding on your court—but it can still be useful, especially when your jurisdiction has not decided the issue or when the reasoning is particularly strong.

- **Lower courts**

  What this means: A lower court's decision (for example, a trial-court order or a lower appellate court) may persuade another court, but it does not control a higher court. Lower-court cases are most helpful when they are well-reasoned and closely aligned with your facts.

- **Sibling circuits**

  What this means: In federal court, a "sibling circuit" is another U.S. Court of Appeals outside your circuit. Those decisions are not binding, but courts often consider them—especially when there is no controlling authority or when multiple circuits agree on the same rule.

- **Secondary sources**

  What are secondary sources? Secondary sources are materials that **explain, summarize, or analyze** the law rather than create it. Common examples include the *Restatements*, treatises (e.g., practice-focused books), law review articles, ALR annotations, bar association guides, and practice manuals. They are generally **persuasive**, not binding.

  Where do you find secondary sources? You often discover them in two places: (1) **inside the opinion**, when the court cites a secondary source in the text or in a citation string (for example, citing a Restatement section or a treatise to explain a rule); and (2) **outside the opinion**, by checking the case's "cited by"/"citing references" list (e.g., on Google Scholar) to find later cases and articles discussing the decision.

  Mini example (as it might appear in an opinion): The court explained the duty standard by referencing the Restatement. *(Example cite) Restatement (Second) of Torts* § 323 (Am. L. Inst. 1965).

Example: A case from one federal court of appeals is generally persuasive (not binding) in a different federal court of appeals.

Understanding citations means understanding power.

7. How to Cite Statutes

Statutes have their own architecture.

Example (federal): **28 U.S.C. § 1332**

Breakdown:

- 28 = title number
- U.S.C. = United States Code
- § = section
- 1332 = section number

Example (state): **[STATE] Stat. § [SECTION]**

Always check your jurisdiction's citation rules and use the court's preferred abbreviation for your state's statutes.

8. How to Cite Regulations

Federal regulations:

29 C.F.R. § 1602.14

Breakdown:

- 29 = title
- C.F.R. = Code of Federal Regulations
- § 1602.14 = section

9. Parentheticals: The Secret Weapon of Persuasion

Parentheticals explain why a case matters.

Example: ***Smith v. Jones***, 912 F.3d 123, 130 ([CIRCUIT] Cir. [YEAR]) (holding that voluntary undertakings create a duty of care)

Types of parentheticals:

- (holding that…)
- (finding that…)

- (explaining that…)
- (noting that…)
- (distinguishing…)
- (emphasis added)

Parentheticals are mini-arguments.

10. Italics: The Professional Touch

Always italicize:

- case names
- citation signals (e.g., *Id., supra, infra*, see, cf.)
- defined terms – but only the first time you introduce them

Never italicize:

- reporter abbreviations (F.3d, S. Ct.,U.S.)
- court names (D. Mass., 7th Cir.)
- statute numbers (§ 1983, 28 U.S.C. § 1332)

Important distinctions:

- Only the **case name** is italicized — the rest of the citation stays in regular font.
- Short-from case names are also italicized: *Johnson,* 455 F.Supp.3d at 118.
- *Id.* Is capitalized only when it begins a citation sentence: otherwise, use *id.*

11. Putting It All Together: A Model Citation Section

Here is a fully formatted example:

Johnson v. Metro Co., 455 F. Supp. 3d 112, 118 ([DISTRICT] [YEAR]) (holding that a defendant who undertakes responsibility for another's safety owes a duty of care)

This is the level of clarity and confidence your reader will gain.

CHAPTER EIGHT

Researching the Law Without Proprietary Tools

How to Find, Read, Understand & Use Cases Using Accessible, Public Sources

Legal research is often treated as a mysterious skill reserved for those with access to expensive databases. But the truth is this:

This chapter gives you the tools to research confidently using **publicly available sources**, and to understand the architecture of legal authority no matter where you find it.

1. What Legal Research Really Is

Legal research is not about searching. It is about **finding the rule that governs your issue**.

Every research task has three goals:

1. **Identify the legal issue**
2. **Find the governing rule**
3. **Find cases that interpret or apply that rule**

Everything else is detail.

2. Where You Can Research Without Proprietary Tools

You can conduct meaningful research using:

A. Google Scholar (Case Law Section)

- Free
- Searchable by jurisdiction
- Provides full opinions
- Allows keyword searching
- Shows citing references

B. State Court Websites

Many states publish:

- opinions
- dockets
- orders
- rules

C. Federal Court Websites

PACER requires payment, but many federal courts publish:

- opinions
- orders
- local rules

D. Government Websites

For statutes and regulations:

- **U.S. Code** (govinfo.gov)
- **Code of Federal Regulations**
- **State statutes** (official state sites)

E. Secondary Sources (Free)

- Law review articles (SSRN, university repositories)
- Legal blogs (for general understanding, not authority)
- Bar association guides

You do not always need expensive tools to do research.

3. How to Begin a Research Assignment

Every research task begins with one question:

"What is the legal issue?"

To find it, ask:

- What happened?
- What law might apply?
- What is the client asking?
- What is the supervisor asking?
- What is the dispute about?

Once you know the issue, you can begin searching.

4. How to Search Effectively

A. Use Keywords Strategically

Combine:

- legal terms
- factual terms
- jurisdiction

Example: "voluntary undertaking duty of care [STATE]"

B. Use Quotation Marks for Exact Phrases

"voluntary undertaking doctrine"

C. Use Connectors

- AND
- OR
- NOT

D. Use Jurisdiction Filters

Always narrow by:

- state
- federal circuit
- court level

E. Use Citing References

If you find one good case, look at:

- cases that cite it
- cases it cites

This is how you build a chain of authority.

5. How to Read a Case Like a Lawyer

Every case has the same architecture:

A. Caption

Tells you the parties.

B. Procedural Posture

Tells you how the case got to this court.

C. Facts

Tells you what happened.

D. Issue

The legal question.

E. Rule

The governing law.

F. Application (Reasoning)

How the court applied the rule to the facts.

G. Holding

The answer to the issue.

H. Disposition

What the court did (affirmed, reversed, remanded).

Once you learn this structure, you can read any case.

6. How to Extract the Rule From a Case

The rule is usually found in:

- the issue statement
- the rule section
- the reasoning
- the holding

A rule may be:

- a statute
- a regulation
- a common-law principle
- a test (e.g., “three-part test”)
- a standard (e.g., “reasonable person”)

Your job is to **state the rule clearly in your own words**.

7. How to Brief a Case for a Supervising Attorney

This is the section that saves new associates.

A case brief for a supervisor must be:

- clear
- concise
- accurate

- neutral
- structured

A. Case Name (italicized) & Citation

Johnson v. Metro Co., 455 F. Supp. 3d 112 ([DISTRICT] [YEAR])

B. Procedural Posture

Explain how the case arrived at this court.

C. Facts

Only the legally relevant facts.

D. Issue

State the legal question.

E. Rule

State the governing rule.

F. Holding

State the court's answer.

G. Reasoning

Explain why the court ruled that way.

H. Notes for the Supervisor

- How this case helps
- How it hurts
- How it compares to other cases
- Any open questions

8. How to Deliver a Research Summary to a Supervisor

A research summary should include:

- the issue
- the governing rule
- the best cases
- how those cases apply
- any conflicting authority
- your conclusion

It should be:

- organized
- neutral
- complete
- easy to skim

Supervisors want clarity, not volume.

9. The Researcher's Mindset

You are not searching for "the right answer." You are searching for:

- the rule
- the cases
- the reasoning
- the pattern

Legal research is pattern recognition.

Once you see the pattern, you understand the law.

CHAPTER NINE

How to Brief a Case for a Supervising Attorney

A Practical, Professional Blueprint for Delivering Case Analysis That Partners Trust

Briefing a case for a supervising attorney is different from briefing a case for law school. In law school, case briefs are teaching tools. In practice, case briefs are **decision tools**.

A supervising attorney wants:

- clarity
- accuracy
- relevance
- brevity
- insight

They want to know:

- what the case says
- how it applies
- whether it helps or hurts
- how it fits into the larger legal landscape

This chapter teaches you exactly how to deliver that.

1. The Purpose of a Practice-Ready Case Brief

A case brief for a supervising attorney is not an academic exercise. It is a **professional product**.

Its purpose is to:

- summarize the case

- extract the rule
- explain the reasoning
- identify the holding
- evaluate its usefulness
- connect it to the assignment

A good case brief saves your supervisor time. A great case brief earns their trust.

2. The Architecture of a Practice Case Brief

A practice case brief has eight essential components:

1. **Case Name (italicized) & Citation**
2. **Court & Year**
3. **Procedural Posture**
4. **Facts (Legally Relevant Only)**
5. **Issue**
6. **Rule**
7. **Holding & Reasoning**
8. **Notes for the Supervisor**

Each part has a purpose. Each part is a structural beam in the analysis.

Let's break them down like an architect.

3. Case Name (italicized) & Citation

Example: ***Johnson v. Metro Co.***, 455 F. Supp. 3d 112 ([DISTRICT] [YEAR])

This tells your supervisor:

- the parties
- the reporter
- the court
- the year

It is the "address" of the case.

4. Court & Year

Even if included in the citation, restating it helps the reader.

Example (federal) (example): United States District Court for the [DISTRICT] ([YEAR]).

This tells your supervisor:

- the jurisdiction
- the authority level
- whether the case is binding or persuasive

5. Procedural Posture

Procedural posture answers:

- How did this case get here?
- What motion is being decided?
- What stage is the case in?

Examples:

- "Appeal from summary judgment."
- "Motion to dismiss."
- "Bench trial verdict."
- "Interlocutory appeal."

Procedural posture shapes the standard of review — which shapes the outcome.

6. Facts (Only the Legally Relevant Ones)

Do **not** retell the entire story. Do **not** include emotional or irrelevant details.

Include only:

- facts necessary to understand the issue
- facts the court relied on
- facts that matter to your assignment

This section should be:

- neutral
- concise
- chronological

Think of it as the **foundation** of the case.

7. Issue (The Legal Question)

The issue is the question the court must answer.

Example: "Did the defendant owe a duty of care under the voluntary-undertaking doctrine?"

A good issue statement is:

- clear
- neutral
- specific
- answerable

The issue is the **hinge** of the case.

8. Rule (The Governing Law)

This is the legal principle the court applies.

It may come from:

- a statute
- a regulation
- a prior case
- a multi-factor test
- a standard (e.g., "reasonable person")

State the rule in your own words unless the exact language is essential.

The rule is the **beam** that supports the analysis.

9. Holding & Reasoning

This is the heart of the case brief.

A. Holding

The court's answer to the issue.

B. Reasoning

Why the court reached that answer.

Include:

- how the court interpreted the rule
- how the court applied the rule to the facts
- how the court distinguished other cases
- any policy considerations

This is where you show your supervisor you understand the case.

10. Notes for the Supervisor (Your Secret Weapon)

This is the section that turns a student brief into a professional brief.

Include:

A. How the Case Helps

- Does it support our argument?
- Does it establish a favorable rule?

B. How the Case Hurts

- Does it contain unfavorable language?
- Does it support the opposing side?

C. How It Fits Into the Larger Landscape

- Is it binding?
- Is it persuasive?
- Is it distinguishable?

D. Any Open Questions

- Ambiguities
- Conflicting authority
- Unresolved issues

This section shows judgment — the skill supervisors value most.

11. A Full Example of a Practice-Ready Case Brief

Below is a model you can use in your own work.

***Johnson v. Metro Co.*, 455 F. Supp. 3d 112 ([DISTRICT] [YEAR])**

Court & Year: [COURT NAME] ([YEAR]).

Procedural Posture: Motion for summary judgment filed by the defendant.

Facts: The defendant inspected scaffolding at a construction site, assured the plaintiff it was secure, and instructed him to proceed. The scaffolding collapsed, injuring the plaintiff.

Issue: Did the defendant owe a duty of care under the voluntary-undertaking doctrine?

Rule: A party who voluntarily undertakes responsibility for another's safety must exercise reasonable care in performing that undertaking.

Holding & Reasoning: Yes. The defendant assumed responsibility by inspecting the scaffolding and assuring the plaintiff it was safe. The plaintiff relied on these assurances. Under established precedent, such conduct creates a duty of care.

Notes for the Supervisor:

- **Helps:** Strong authority supporting voluntary-undertaking liability.
- **Hurts:** Court notes that reliance must be reasonable; opposing counsel may argue reliance was not reasonable here.
- **Authority Level:** Persuasive in our jurisdiction but not binding.
- **Open Questions:** Court did not address comparative negligence; may need additional research.

12. Delivering the Brief to Your Supervisor

When submitting your brief:

- use clear headings
- keep paragraphs short
- avoid legalese

- attach the case if requested
- include a short summary in the email

Your goal is to make your supervisor's job easier.

CHAPTER TEN

The Architecture of Motions & Briefs

A Line-by-Line Blueprint for Building Court-Ready Documents

A motion or brief is not a creative exercise. It is a **constructed object** — a legal building made of required parts, governed by rules, and designed to guide the judge from the front door (the caption) to the final request for relief.

Template notice (read before using): The examples and templates in Chapters Ten and Eleven are designed as a non-jurisdiction-specific starting point. They are not filing-ready forms. Before using any template, confirm the applicable rules and requirements in your jurisdiction, including local rules, standing orders, page limits, formatting rules, and service/filing procedures. Replace all bracketed placeholders (e.g., "[COURT NAME]") with jurisdiction-specific information and confirm statutory and rule citations.

This chapter teaches you how to build that structure with precision, confidence, and professional clarity.

1. The Motion or Brief as a Building

Every legal document has:

- a **foundation** (caption)
- a **front door** (title)
- a **foyer** (introduction)
- a **floor plan** (table of contents, if required)
- **rooms** (sections)
- **support beams** (headings)
- **walls** (paragraphs)

- a **roof** (conclusion)
- a **seal** (signature block)
- a **delivery record** (certificate of service)

Once you see the structure, you can build anything.

2. The Caption — The Document's Address Plate

The caption is a highly regulated part of the document. It is governed by:

- federal rules
- state rules
- local rules
- judge-specific rules

Purpose

To identify:

- the court
- the parties
- the case number
- the judge (if required)
- the document being filed

Architectural Breakdown

IN THE [COURT NAME]

[DIVISION / DISTRICT / COUNTY, IF APPLICABLE]

[PLAINTIFF NAME],)

Plaintiff,)

)

v.) Case No. [CASE NUMBER]

)

[DEFENDANT NAME],)

Defendant.)

[Caption formats vary significantly by court (trial vs. appellate; state vs. federal). Use this layout only as a structural guide and conform your caption to the controlling rules and any court-provided caption form.]

Why It Matters

The caption is the **address** of your legal building. If it is wrong, the court may reject the filing.

3. The Title of the Document — The Blueprint Label

Examples:

- **PLAINTIFF'S MOTION FOR SUMMARY JUDGMENT**
- **DEFENDANT'S BRIEF IN SUPPORT OF MOTION TO DISMISS**

Purpose

To tell the judge exactly what you want.

Architectural Role

This is the **label on the blueprint** — it tells the court what structure you are presenting.

4. The Introduction — The Foyer of the Document

The introduction is where you orient the judge.

Purpose

- State what you want
- State why you are entitled to it
- Provide a roadmap

Example

"Plaintiff respectfully moves for summary judgment because the undisputed facts show that Defendant voluntarily undertook responsibility for Plaintiff's safety and breached that duty."

Architectural Role

The **foyer** — the judge steps inside and immediately understands the layout.

5. The Statement of Facts — The Site Survey

The facts must be:

- neutral
- accurate
- chronological
- relevant

Purpose

To give the judge the factual landscape before legal analysis begins.

Architectural Role

The **site survey** — the terrain on which the legal building stands.

6. The Standard of Review — The Building Code

The standard of review tells the judge:

- how to evaluate the motion
- what level of deference applies
- what the moving party must show

Examples:

- **Motion to Dismiss:** Court accepts all well-pleaded facts as true.
- **Summary Judgment:** No genuine dispute of material fact.

Architectural Role

The **building code** — the rules that govern construction.

7. The Argument Section — The Structural Framework

This is the heart of the document.

Each argument point is a **support beam**. If one beam is weak, the structure collapses.

Each Point Heading Must Be a Complete Sentence

Example:

I. Defendant Owed a Duty of Care Because He Voluntarily Undertook Responsibility for Plaintiff's Safety.

Structure of Each Argument Point

Use CREAC or CRuPAC:

1. **Conclusion (heading)**
2. **Rule**
3. **Explanation of the rule**
4. **Application**
5. **Mini-conclusion**

Architectural Role

The **framing** — beams, joists, supports.

8. Headings — The Beams That Hold the Structure

Headings must:

- be complete sentences
- state the legal conclusion
- guide the judge
- break the argument into digestible pieces

Example of Strong Headings

I. Defendant Owed a Duty of Care Under the Voluntary-Undertaking Doctrine.

II. Defendant Breached That Duty by Failing to Secure the Scaffolding.

III. Plaintiff's Injuries Were the Foreseeable Result of Defendant's Breach.

Architectural Role

The **load-bearing beams**.

9. Paragraphs — The Walls of the Structure

Each paragraph must:

- begin with a topic sentence
- contain one idea
- follow CREAC logic
- end with a mini-conclusion

Architectural Role

The **walls** — they define the rooms and guide movement.

10. The Conclusion — The Roof

The conclusion is short and direct.

Purpose

To state the relief requested.

Example

"For the foregoing reasons, Plaintiff respectfully requests that this Court grant summary judgment in his favor."

Architectural Role

The **roof** — it completes the structure.

11. The Signature Block — The Architect's Seal

Includes:

- attorney name
- bar number
- firm
- address
- phone
- email

Architectural Role

The **seal** — your professional certification.

12. Certificate of Service — Proof of Delivery

Required in most jurisdictions.

Purpose

To confirm that all parties received the document.

Architectural Role

The **delivery record** — proof the plans were sent to all stakeholders.

CHAPTER ELEVEN

Annotated Sample Motions, Briefs & Memorandums

Blueprints in Action — Fully Labeled, Line-by-Line Examples of Court-Ready Legal Documents

You have learned the architecture. You have learned the rules. You have learned the structure, the purpose, and the logic behind every part of a legal document.

Now it is time to **see the entire building assembled**.

This chapter provides:

- a **fully annotated motion**
- a **fully annotated memorandum**
- a **fully annotated brief**

Each sample is:

- formatted according to common federal conventions
- labeled like a blueprint
- explained line by line
- designed to show you *why* each part exists
- written in clean, professional, court-ready prose

These are not templates to memorize. They are **models** — teaching tools that reveal the internal logic of legal writing.

SECTION ONE — ANNOTATED SAMPLE MOTION

Motion for Summary Judgment

CAPTION

[Caption requirements vary by court. Use this as a structural starting point only. Conform your caption to the applicable rules, local rules, and standing orders, and replace all bracketed placeholders.]

Note: [Continue caption formatting per local rules.]

[CAPTION BLOCK CONTINUES]

IN THE [COURT NAME]

[DIVISION / DISTRICT / COUNTY, IF APPLICABLE]

[PLAINTIFF NAME],)

Plaintiff,)

)

v.) Case No. [CASE NUMBER]

)

[DEFENDANT NAME],)

Defendant.)

[Caption notes: Some courts limit party names in the caption (e.g., first-named parties + *et al.*). Follow local rules for spacing, alignment, and parenthesis lines.]

TITLE OF DOCUMENT

PLAINTIFF'S MOTION FOR SUMMARY JUDGMENT [The

title must clearly state what relief is sought.]

INTRODUCTION

[This is the "foyer" — orient the judge immediately.]

Plaintiff [PLAINTIFF NAME] respectfully moves for summary judgment because the undisputed facts show that Defendant [DEFENDANT NAME] voluntarily undertook responsibility for Plaintiff's safety and breached that duty, causing Plaintiff's injuries. [States the relief and the reason.]

STATEMENT OF FACTS

[Neutral, chronological, relevant.]

On [DATE], Defendant's site supervisor inspected the scaffolding at the construction site and assured Plaintiff that it was secure. Plaintiff relied on this assurance and proceeded to work on the platform. Minutes later, the scaffolding collapsed, causing Plaintiff to fall and sustain serious injuries. [Only legally relevant facts. No emotion. No argument.]

STANDARD OF REVIEW

[The "building code."]

Example (federal): Summary judgment is appropriate when "there is no genuine dispute as to any material fact and the movant is entitled to judgment as a matter of law." Fed. R. Civ. P. 56(a). [If filing in state court, substitute the applicable state rule and controlling case law.]

ARGUMENT

[This is a **trial-court motion** example (Plaintiff/Defendant). For an **appellate-brief** excerpt with Appellant/Appellee terminology and a Preliminary Statement/Summary of Argument, see **Section Three**.]

I. DEFENDANT OWED PLAINTIFF A DUTY OF CARE

UNDER THE VOLUNTARY-UNDERTAKING DOCTRINE.

[The structural framework — each point is a support beam.]

A. Defendant owed a duty because it invited reliance by affirmatively assuring safety.

[Headings must be complete sentences.]

Rule: A party who voluntarily undertakes responsibility for another's safety must exercise reasonable care in performing that undertaking. [State the rule clearly.]

Explanation: Courts impose this duty when a defendant's assurances create foreseeable reliance. [Explain the rule in your own words.]

Application: Here, Defendant inspected the scaffolding and assured Plaintiff it was safe. Plaintiff relied on that assurance. [Apply the rule to the facts.]

Mini-Conclusion: Therefore, Defendant owed Plaintiff a duty of care. [Close the loop.]

II. Defendant Breached That Duty by Failing to Secure the Scaffolding.

Rule: A breach occurs when a party fails to exercise reasonable care.

Application: Defendant's inspection was inadequate, and the scaffolding collapsed minutes later.

Mini-Conclusion: Defendant breached the duty of care.

III. Plaintiff's Injuries Were the Foreseeable Result of Defendant's Breach.

Rule: A defendant is liable for harm that is the foreseeable result of their negligence.

Application: A fall from unsecured scaffolding is a foreseeable consequence of failing to ensure its stability.

Mini-Conclusion: Plaintiff's injuries were proximately caused by Defendant's breach.

CONCLUSION

[The roof.]

For the foregoing reasons, Plaintiff respectfully requests that this Court grant summary judgment in his favor. [Short, direct, professional.]

SIGNATURE BLOCK

[The architect's seal.]

Respectfully submitted,

/s/ [ATTORNEY NAME]

[ATTORNEY NAME]

(Bar No. [BAR NO.], if applicable)

Counsel for [PARTY NAME]

[FIRM / ORGANIZATION]

[ADDRESS LINE 1]

[CITY, STATE ZIP]

[PHONE]

[EMAIL]

CERTIFICATE OF SERVICE

[Proof of delivery.]

I certify that on [DATE], I served the foregoing motion on all counsel of record by [METHOD OF SERVICE] (e.g., the court's electronic filing system, email as permitted, or U.S. mail), in accordance with the applicable rules.

/s/ [ATTORNEY NAME]

SECTION TWO — ANNOTATED SAMPLE MEMORANDUM

Internal Memorandum for a Supervising Attorney

TO / FROM / DATE / RE:

TO: [SUPERVISING ATTORNEY NAME]

FROM: [AUTHOR NAME]

DATE: [DATE]

RE: [SUBJECT] (example: Duty of Care Under Voluntary-Undertaking Doctrine)

[Internal memos always begin with this block.]

QUESTION PRESENTED

[The issue.]

Whether a defendant who inspects equipment and assures a worker that it is safe owes a duty of care under the voluntary-undertaking doctrine. [Neutral, specific, answerable.]

BRIEF ANSWER

[One paragraph. Clear. Direct.]

Yes. Courts hold that a defendant who voluntarily undertakes responsibility for another's safety owes a duty of care when the plaintiff relies on that undertaking. Here, Defendant inspected the scaffolding and assured Plaintiff it was secure, creating a duty. [This is the supervisor's favorite section.]

FACTS

[Neutral, relevant.]

(Same as motion.)

DISCUSSION

[Use CREAC.]

Conclusion: Defendant owed a duty of care.

Rule: A party who undertakes responsibility for another's safety must exercise reasonable care.

Explanation: Courts impose this duty when a defendant's assurances create foreseeable reliance.

Application: Defendant inspected the scaffolding and assured Plaintiff it was safe. Plaintiff relied on that assurance.

Conclusion: Defendant owed a duty of care.

CONCLUSION

Defendant owed a duty of care under the voluntary-undertaking doctrine.

SECTION THREE — ANNOTATED SAMPLE BRIEF (APPELLATE BRIEF EXCERPT)

This sample is organized in a common appellate brief order for learning purposes. Appellate rules vary by jurisdiction and court, so confirm the required sections, formatting, and sequence before filing. Some courts also require a **Jurisdictional Statement** and/or a **separate Standard of Review for each issue** (rather than one global standard-of-review section).

APPELLATE CAPTION / COVER (VARIES BY COURT)

[Appellate captions differ significantly. Typical items include: court name, parties (Appellant/Appellee), appeal number, lower-court case number, and the court/judge appealed from. Use the court's required caption form.]

TABLE OF CONTENTS / TABLE OF AUTHORITIES (IF REQUIRED)

[Many appellate courts require a table of contents and table of authorities. These are usually finalized after the brief is complete, because headings and citations must match the finished argument.]

STATEMENT OF ISSUES PRESENTED

1. Whether the trial court erred in granting summary judgment where Appellee's site supervisor inspected the scaffolding, assured Appellant it was secure, and Appellant relied on that undertaking before the platform collapsed. [Record citations.]

STATEMENT OF THE CASE (PROCEDURAL HISTORY)

This appeal arises from the trial court's order granting summary judgment to Appellee on [DATE]. [Record citation.] Appellant timely filed a notice of appeal on [DATE]. [Record citation.]

STATEMENT OF FACTS

On [DATE], Appellee's site supervisor inspected the scaffolding and told Appellant it was secure. [Record citation.] Appellant proceeded to work on the platform in reliance on that assurance. [Record citation.] Minutes later, the platform collapsed, and Appellant suffered injuries. [Record citation.]

STANDARD OF REVIEW

The appellate court reviews a grant of summary judgment de novo. See [CONTROLLING SUMMARY-JUDGMENT AUTHORITY]. Summary judgment is improper where genuine disputes of material fact remain. See [CONTROLLING SUMMARY-JUDGMENT AUTHORITY].

SUMMARY OF ARGUMENT (PRELIMINARY STATEMENT)

The trial court's duty ruling was error. Under the voluntary-undertaking doctrine, a party who undertakes to render services for the protection of another must exercise reasonable care when the undertaking invites reliance or increases the risk of harm. See [CONTROLLING AUTHORITY]. Appellee's supervisor inspected the scaffolding, assured Appellant it was secure, and invited Appellant to proceed—facts that support a duty as a matter of law or, at minimum, create a triable issue.

In any event, summary judgment should have been denied because genuine disputes of material fact remain regarding the scope of the undertaking, the reasonableness of Appellant's reliance, and whether Appellee's conduct increased the risk of harm. [Record citations.] Those disputes must be resolved by the factfinder, not on summary judgment.

ARGUMENT

I. THE TRIAL COURT ERRED BECAUSE APPELLEE OWED A DUTY UNDER THE VOLUNTARY-UNDERTAKING DOCTRINE.

A. Appellee owed a duty because it invited reliance by affirmatively assuring safety.

Under the voluntary-undertaking doctrine, a person who undertakes to render services for the protection of another must exercise reasonable care in performing that undertaking. See [CONTROLLING AUTHORITY] (recognizing liability where (1) the undertaking increases the risk of harm or (2) the harm results from reliance on the undertaking). Although wording differs by jurisdiction, the core principle is consistent: a defendant cannot invite reliance on a safety assurance and then disclaim responsibility as a matter of law.

Here, the record shows that Appellee's site supervisor inspected the scaffolding and told Appellant it was secure. [Record citation.] Appellant relied on that assurance by proceeding to work on the platform. [Record citation.] The platform then collapsed minutes later, causing Appellant's injuries. [Record citation.] These facts support a finding that Appellee undertook responsibility for Appellant's safety and that Appellant relied on the undertaking—facts that establish duty or, at minimum, create a triable issue for the factfinder. Accordingly, the trial court erred in concluding that no duty existed as a matter of law.

II. IN ANY EVENT, GENUINE DISPUTES OF MATERIAL FACT PRECLUDED SUMMARY JUDGMENT.

Even if the duty analysis turns on context-dependent considerations, summary judgment is improper where the record contains competing evidence on material facts—such as the scope of Appellee's undertaking, the reasonableness of Appellant's reliance, and whether Appellee's conduct increased the risk of harm. [Record citations.]

Those disputed facts must be resolved by the factfinder, not on summary judgment. See [CONTROLLING SUMMARY-JUDGMENT AUTHORITY].

CONCLUSION

For the foregoing reasons, Appellant respectfully requests that this Court reverse the judgment below and remand for further proceedings. [Or other relief required by the assignment and rules.]

SIGNATURE BLOCK

Respectfully submitted,

/s/ [ATTORNEY NAME]

[ATTORNEY NAME]

(Bar No. [BAR NO.], if required)

Counsel for Appellant: [ATTORNEY NAME],

[FIRM / ORGANIZATION],

[ADDRESS],

[PHONE],

[EMAIL]

CERTIFICATE OF SERVICE

I certify that on [DATE], I served this brief on all counsel of record by [METHOD OF SERVICE] (e.g., the court's electronic filing system, email as permitted, or U.S. mail), in accordance with the applicable rules.

CERTIFICATE OF COMPLIANCE (IF REQUIRED)

I certify that this brief complies with the applicable [WORD

COUNT / PAGE LIMIT] because it contains [WORD COUNT] words, excluding the parts exempted by rule. I further certify that this brief complies with the typeface and formatting requirements of [APPLICABLE RULE].

SECTION FOUR — ANNOTATED DEMAND LETTER

Pre-Litigation Demand for Compensation (Fully Annotated)

LETTERHEAD / FIRM INFORMATION

[Professional letters always begin with firm information.]

Law Firm LLP

123 Main Street

New York, NY 10001

(212) 555-1234

jattorney@lawfirm.com

DATE

March 18, 2026 [Always include the date for record-keeping.]

RECIPIENT INFORMATION

Metro Co.

Attn: Claims Department

456 Industrial Way

New York, NY 10002

[Address the letter to the correct department or individual.]

RE: Demand for Compensation — John Doe Injury Claim

[Clear subject line. Professional. Specific.]

SALUTATION

Dear Claims Representative: [Neutral and professional.]

OPENING PARAGRAPH — PURPOSE OF LETTER

This firm represents John Doe regarding injuries he sustained on March 12, 2023, at your construction site. We write to demand compensation for the harm caused by Metro Co.'s negligence. [State representation + purpose immediately.]

FACTUAL SUMMARY

On March 12, 2023, your site supervisor inspected the scaffolding and assured Mr. Doe that it was secure. Relying on this assurance, Mr. Doe proceeded to work on the platform. The scaffolding collapsed minutes later, causing him to fall and suffer significant injuries. [Neutral, concise, relevant.]

LIABILITY STATEMENT

Metro Co. is liable under the voluntary-undertaking doctrine because your supervisor assumed responsibility for Mr. Doe's safety and failed to exercise reasonable care in performing that undertaking. [One paragraph establishing liability.]

DAMAGES SUMMARY

As a result of your company's negligence, Mr. Doe suffered:

- medical expenses totaling $48,500
- lost wages of $12,000
- ongoing physical therapy costs
- pain and suffering

[Bullet points make damages easy to read.]

DEMAND

Accordingly, we demand payment of **$150,000** to resolve this matter without litigation. [Clear, firm, specific.]

DEADLINE

Please respond within **14 days** of the date of this letter. If we do not receive a satisfactory response, we will proceed with litigation. [Deadlines create urgency.]

CLOSING

We look forward to your prompt attention to this matter.

Sincerely,

/s/ Jane Attorney

Attorney for John Doe

SECTION FIVE — ANNOTATED CLIENT LETTER

Explaining Case Status to a Client

LETTERHEAD

(Same as above.)

DATE

March 18, 2026

RECIPIENT INFORMATION

John Doe

789 Park Avenue

New York, NY 10003

RE: Update on Your Case — Doe v. Metro Co.

SALUTATION

Dear Mr. Doe:

OPENING — PURPOSE OF LETTER

I am writing to update you on the status of your case against Metro Co. and to explain the next steps in the process. [Clients need clarity and reassurance.]

SUMMARY OF RECENT DEVELOPMENT

On March 10, 2026, we filed your Motion for Summary Judgment. This motion asks the court to rule in your favor without a trial because the key facts are undisputed. [Explain legal terms in plain English.]

WHAT HAPPENS NEXT

Metro Co. has until April 5, 2026, to file its response. After that, the court may schedule oral argument or decide the motion based on the written submissions. [Clients need timelines.]

YOUR RESPONSIBILITIES

At this stage, you do not need to take any action. If the court schedules a hearing, I will notify you immediately. [Clients appreciate clarity about what they must do.]

REASSURANCE & PROFESSIONAL TONE

Please know that we are monitoring your case closely and will continue to advocate for the best possible outcome. [Professional reassurance.]

CLOSING

If you have any questions, please feel free to contact me.

Sincerely,

/s/ Jane Attorney

Jane Attorney for John Doe

CHAPTER TWELVE

Working With Supervising Attorneys

How to Communicate, Deliver Work, and Build Trust in Legal Practice

Legal writing is only half of the job. The other half — is **working with supervising attorneys**.

This chapter gives you the tools to:

- understand expectations
- communicate clearly
- deliver work that builds trust
- handle feedback professionally
- manage deadlines
- ask the right questions
- avoid common pitfalls

This is the chapter that transforms you from a good writer into a reliable, confident legal professional.

1. The Purpose of a Supervising Attorney

A supervising attorney is:

- your teacher
- your evaluator
- your editor
- your protector
- your gateway to professional growth

Their job is to guide you. Your job is to make their job easier.

This is not about hierarchy — it is about **collaboration**.

2. Understanding Expectations (The Unspoken Rules)

Supervising attorneys expect:

- clarity
- accuracy
- professionalism
- timeliness
- judgment
- initiative

They do **not** expect perfection. They expect reliability.

The fastest way to build trust is to:

- ask clarifying questions
- deliver clean drafts
- meet deadlines
- communicate early if issues arise

These habits matter more than brilliance.

3. How to Receive an Assignment (The Blueprint Meeting)

When you receive an assignment, your goal is to understand:

- **the issue**
- **the purpose**
- **the audience**
- **the format**
- **the deadline**

- **the scope**

Here are the questions you should ask:

A. What is the legal issue?

This shapes your research.

B. What is the purpose of the assignment?

Memo? Motion? Email summary?

C. Who is the audience?

Partner? Client? Court?

D. What format should I use?

Internal memo? CREAC? Full brief?

E. What is the deadline?

Always confirm the timeline.

F. How deep should the research go?

One case? A full survey? Just the leading authority?

G. Are there preferred sources?

Some firms prefer certain jurisdictions or databases.

Asking these questions shows professionalism, not insecurity.

4. How to Deliver Work (The Professional Standard)

When you submit work, it should be:

- clean
- organized
- proofread
- formatted correctly

- cited properly
- accompanied by a short summary

Always include a cover email or memo that states:

- what you were asked to do
- what you found
- your conclusion
- any open questions

This makes your supervisor's job easier — and they will remember that.

5. How to Handle Feedback (Without Shame)

Feedback is not criticism. Feedback is training.

Supervising attorneys expect to edit your work. They expect to correct you. They expect to guide you.

Your job is to:

- listen
- take notes
- ask clarifying questions
- apply the feedback next time

Never take edits personally. Edits are a sign that your supervisor is investing in you.

6. How to Ask Questions (The Right Way)

Good questions:

- are specific
- show you've tried to solve the issue

- move the work forward

Example of a strong question:

"I found two cases that interpret the statute differently. Would you prefer I follow the majority approach or highlight the split?"

Example of a weak question:

"I'm confused. What should I do?"

The difference is preparation.

7. How to Manage Deadlines (Your Professional Reputation)

Your reputation is built on:

- meeting deadlines
- communicating early
- never surprising your supervisor

If you need more time:

- tell them early
- explain why
- propose a new timeline

Supervisors appreciate honesty and planning.

8. How to Handle Uncertainty (The Judgment Skill)

Lawyers deal with ambiguity every day. Your supervisor wants to see that you can:

- identify uncertainty
- explain it
- propose solutions

Example:

"The case law is split. I recommend relying on the Second Circuit's approach because it aligns with our facts."

This shows judgment — a valued skill in practice.

9. How to Communicate Professionally

Professional communication is:

- concise
- respectful
- clear
- timely

Avoid:

- long emails
- emotional language
- assumptions
- silence

Use:

- bullet points
- headings
- summaries
- clear requests

Your writing style becomes your professional identity.

10. How to Follow Up (Without Being a Burden)

Follow up when:

- a deadline is approaching
- you need clarification
- you completed the task
- you found something important

Do **not** follow up excessively. Do **not** send multiple emails in a row. Do **not** assume urgency unless stated.

11. How to Build Trust Over Time

Trust is built through:

- consistency
- clarity
- reliability
- professionalism
- good judgment

When supervisors trust you, they:

- give you better assignments
- give you more responsibility
- advocate for you
- mentor you
- invest in your growth

CHAPTER THIRTEEN

Templates, Checklists & Practice Exercises

Your Practical Toolkit for Building Legal Writing Mastery

You now understand the architecture of legal writing. You have seen full annotated example.0es. You have learned how to research, analyze, structure, and communicate.

This chapter gives you the **tools** — the templates, checklists, and exercises that turn theory into skill.

These are not rigid forms. They are **starting points**, designed to help you build confidence and consistency as you grow into your own legal writing voice.

SECTION ONE — TEMPLATES

Blueprint-Style Templates for Real-World Legal Writing

Each template is written in clean, professional language and structured according to the architectural principles you've learned.

1. Motion Template (General Federal Format)

[CAPTION]

[Title of Document]

INTRODUCTION

[One paragraph stating what you want and why.]

STATEMENT OF FACTS

[Neutral, chronological, relevant.]

STANDARD OF REVIEW

[State the governing rule.]

ARGUMENT

I. [Heading stating the legal conclusion.]

[Rule]

[Explanation]

[Application]

[Mini-Conclusion]

II. [Second argument point.]

[Same structure.]

CONCLUSION

[State the relief requested.]

[Signature Block]

[Certificate of Service]

2. Internal Memorandum Template

TO:

FROM:

DATE:

RE:

QUESTION PRESENTED

[One sentence, neutral, answerable.]

BRIEF ANSWER

[One paragraph, direct.]

FACTS

[Neutral, relevant.]

DISCUSSION

[Use CREAC or CRuPAC.]

CONCLUSION

[One paragraph.]

3. Demand Letter Template

[Firm Letterhead]

[Date]

[Recipient Name & Address]

RE: [Subject]

Dear [Recipient]:

[Opening paragraph stating purpose.]

[Relevant facts.]

[Liability explanation.]

[Damages summary.]

[Demand.]

[Deadline.]

Sincerely,

[Signature Block]

4. Client Letter Template

[Firm Letterhead]

[Date]

[Client Name & Address]

RE: [Subject]

Dear [Client]:

[Purpose of letter.]

[Summary of recent developments.]

[Next steps.]

[Client responsibilities.]

[Reassurance.]

Sincerely,

[Signature Block]

SECTION TWO — CHECKLISTS

Your Quick-Reference Guides for Every Stage of Writing

These checklists help you avoid common mistakes and ensure your work is polished, professional, and complete.

1. Pre-Writing Checklist

- Do I understand the issue?
- Do I know the purpose of the document?
- Do I know the audience?
- Do I know the deadline?
- Do I know the required format?
- Do I know the jurisdiction?
- Do I know the standard of review?
- Do I know the scope of research needed?

2. Paragraph Checklist

- Does the paragraph have a clear topic sentence?
- Does it contain only one idea?
- Does it follow CREAC logic?
- Does it end with a mini-conclusion?
- Does it transition smoothly to the next paragraph?

3. Argument Section Checklist

- Are the headings complete sentences?
- Does each heading state a legal conclusion?

- Does each point follow CREAC or CRuPAC?
- Are the rules accurate and cited?
- Is the application specific and persuasive?
- Are block quotes used sparingly?
- Is the tone professional and neutral?

4. Editing Checklist

- Have I removed filler words?
- Are sentences clear and concise?
- Is the tone professional?
- Are citations correct?
- Are quotations accurate?
- Are headings consistent?
- Are transitions smooth?
- Is the document formatted according to rules?

5. Submission Checklist

- Did I proofread?
- Did I run spellcheck?
- Did I check citations?
- Did I include a cover email or memo?
- Did I meet the deadline?
- Did I follow instructions exactly?

SECTION THREE — PRACTICE EXERCISES

Exercises That Build Skill Through Repetition and Reflection

These exercises help you internalize the structures and techniques you've learned.

Exercise 1 — Write a CREAC Paragraph

Prompt: Write a CREAC paragraph analyzing whether a store owed a duty of care when a customer slipped on a wet floor.

Goal: Practice structure, clarity, and application.

Exercise 2 — Rewrite for Clarity

Rewrite the following sentence to make it clear and concise:

"It is important to note that the defendant, in this particular instance, failed to adequately warn the plaintiff of the potential dangers that were present at the time."

Goal: Practice conciseness.

Exercise 3 — Draft a Heading

Draft a complete-sentence heading for this argument:

The landlord failed to repair a broken stair despite repeated complaints.

Goal: Practice persuasive headings.

Exercise 4 — Identify the Issue

Given a short fact pattern, identify the legal issue in one sentence.

Goal: Practice issue spotting.

Exercise 5 — Draft a Client Update Email

Write a short, professional email updating a client on the status of their case.

Goal: Practice tone and clarity.

SECTION FOUR — BUILDING YOUR OWN TEMPLATES

As you grow, you will:

- adapt these templates
- refine them
- personalize them
- build new ones

Your templates will become your **professional toolkit** — the tools you reach for when the deadline is tight, the issue is complex, or the stakes are high.

CHAPTER FOURTEEN

Editing Like a Lawyer

How to Revise, Refine, and Polish Your Writing With Professional Precision

Writing is only half the job. Editing is where the real work — and the real transformation — happens.

Lawyers do not submit first drafts. Lawyers submit **edited** drafts — documents that have been shaped, tightened, clarified, and polished until they are clear, credible, and court-ready.

This chapter teaches you how to edit like a lawyer: with structure, discipline, and purpose.

1. Editing Is a Separate Skill From Writing

Writing is creative. Editing is architectural.

Writing builds the structure. Editing strengthens it.

Writing is about ideas. Editing is about clarity.

Writing is the first draft. Editing is the professional draft.

Once you understand this, editing becomes less emotional and more strategic.

2. The Four Layers of Legal Editing

Lawyers edit in layers — never all at once.

Layer 1 — Structure (The Blueprint Check)

Ask:

- Does the document follow the required format?
- Are the sections in the correct order?
- Are the headings complete sentences?

- Does each argument follow CREAC or CRuPAC?

This is the architectural layer.

Layer 2 — Clarity (The Reader Experience Check)

Ask:

- Can the reader understand each sentence on the first read?
- Are topic sentences clear?
- Do paragraphs contain only one idea?
- Are transitions smooth?

This is the readability layer.

Layer 3 — Conciseness (The Tightening Layer)

Ask:

- Can this sentence be shorter?
- Can this phrase be replaced with one word?
- Is there repetition?
- Is there filler?

This is the precision layer.

Layer 4 — Technical Accuracy (The Professional Layer)

Ask:

- Are citations correct?
- Are quotations accurate?
- Are block quotes formatted properly?
- Are names, dates, and facts correct?

This is the credibility layer.

3. The Editing Mindset: Detached, Curious, Professional

Editing requires emotional distance.

You are not judging yourself. You are improving the document.

Approach editing with:

- curiosity ("How can this be clearer?")
- professionalism ("What does the reader need?")
- discipline ("Does this follow the rules?")

Editing is not punishment. Editing is refinement.

4. The Most Common Editing Problems (and How to Fix Them)

A. Long, winding sentences

Fix: Split into two. Use strong verbs.

B. Weak topic sentences

Fix: State the point clearly at the start.

C. Over-quoting

Fix: Summarize in your own words unless exact language is required.

D. Legalese

Fix: Replace archaic terms with plain English.

E. Passive voice overuse

Fix: Use active voice unless passive is necessary.

F. Repetition

Fix: Remove duplicate ideas.

G. Wandering paragraphs

Fix: One idea per paragraph.

H. Missing mini-conclusions

Fix: End each paragraph with a closing sentence.

5. The 10-Step Editing Process (Your Professional Workflow)

Step 1 — Take a break

Distance gives clarity.

Step 2 — Read the document aloud

If you stumble, the reader will too.

Step 3 — Check structure

Does the document follow the blueprint?

Step 4 — Check headings

Do they state legal conclusions?

Step 5 — Check paragraphs

Do they follow CREAC logic?

Step 6 — Check sentences

Are they clear, concise, and direct?

Step 7 — Check citations

Are they accurate and consistent?

Step 8 — Check quotations

Are they formatted correctly?

Step 9 — Check tone

Is it professional, neutral, and credible?

Step 10 — Final proofread

Slow, careful, line by line.

6. Editing Tools Lawyers Use

Lawyers rely on:

- checklists
- templates
- style guides
- jurisdictional rules
- peer review
- reading aloud
- printing and marking up drafts

These tools help ensure consistency and accuracy.

7. Editing for Different Audiences

A. Editing for a Judge

- prioritize clarity
- front-load conclusions
- use strong headings
- avoid unnecessary detail

B. Editing for a Supervising Attorney

- prioritize accuracy
- include relevant cases
- highlight open questions
- be concise

C. Editing for a Client

- use plain English
- avoid legal jargon
- focus on next steps
- be reassuring

Audience determines tone.

8. Before-and-After Editing Examples

Original Sentence:

"It is important to note that the defendant failed to adequately warn the plaintiff of the potential dangers that were present at the time."

Edited Sentence:

"The defendant failed to warn the plaintiff of the danger."

Original Paragraph:

"The defendant owed a duty of care. This is because the defendant undertook responsibility for the plaintiff's safety. Courts have held that when a defendant undertakes responsibility, a duty arises. Therefore, the defendant owed a duty."

Edited Paragraph:

"The defendant owed a duty of care because he voluntarily undertook responsibility for the plaintiff's safety. Courts impose a duty when a defendant's assurances create foreseeable reliance. Here, the defendant inspected the scaffolding and assured the plaintiff it was safe. Therefore, a duty arose."

9. Editing as a Professional Identity

Your editing habits become your reputation.

Lawyers are known for:

- clean writing
- clear structure
- accurate citations
- polished drafts

…are trusted with more responsibility.

Editing is not just a skill. Editing is a **professional identity**.

CHAPTER FIFTEEN

Professional Email Writing for Lawyers

How to Communicate Clearly, Confidently, and Credibly in the Legal Workplace

Email is the dominant form of communication in legal practice. It is how you:

- receive assignments
- deliver work
- communicate with clients
- negotiate with opposing counsel
- coordinate with colleagues
- update supervising attorneys
- manage deadlines
- build your professional reputation

1. Why Email Matters More Than You Think

Your emails are:

- your voice
- your professionalism
- your judgment
- your reliability
- your reputation

Supervising attorneys judge you by your emails long before they see your briefs.

Clients judge your competence by your clarity.

Opposing counsel judge your credibility by your tone.

Email is not administrative. Email is **legal writing**.

2. The Architecture of a Professional Legal Email

Every professional email has the same structure:

1. **Subject Line**
2. **Greeting**
3. **Purpose Sentence**
4. **Body (Clear, concise, structured)**
5. **Next Steps / Requests**
6. **Closing**
7. **Signature Block**

This structure is your blueprint.

3. Subject Lines That Work

A subject line must be:

- clear
- specific
- searchable
- professional

Examples:

- "Draft Memo on Voluntary-Undertaking Doctrine"
- "Summary Judgment Motion — First Draft Attached"
- "Client Update — Doe v. Metro Co."
- "Question About Research Scope"

- "Follow-Up on Assignment"

Avoid vague subject lines like "Hi" or "Quick Question."

4. Greetings That Set the Tone

Use:

- "Hi [Name],"
- "Hello [Name],"
- "Dear [Name]," (commonly used for very formal or senior partners)
- "Good morning/afternoon [Name],"

Avoid overly formal greetings ("Dear Sir") unless writing to a court or unfamiliar counsel.

Avoid overly casual greetings ("Hey!").

5. The Purpose Sentence — Your Reader's Compass

The first sentence should tell the reader **why you are writing**.

Examples:

- "I'm writing to provide the draft memorandum you requested."
- "I have a question about the scope of the research assignment."
- "I'm writing to update you on the status of the motion."

This sentence orients the reader immediately.

6. The Body — Clear, Concise, Structured

Use:

- short paragraphs

- bullet points
- headings (sparingly)
- direct language

Avoid:

- long blocks of text
- emotional language
- unnecessary detail

Example of a strong body paragraph:

"I reviewed the three cases you mentioned. Two support our position, and one is distinguishable because the defendant did not provide any assurances to the plaintiff."

Clear. Direct. Useful.

7. Next Steps — The Navigation Section

Always tell the reader:

- what you need
- what you will do
- what they should expect

Examples:

- "Please let me know if you'd like me to expand the analysis."
- "I will begin drafting the motion unless you prefer a different approach."
- "I can revise this by tomorrow morning if needed."

This shows initiative and professionalism.

8. Closings That Feel Professional

Use:

- "Best,"
- "Regards,"
- "Thank you,"
- "Sincerely," (more formal)

Avoid:

- "Thanks!!!"
- "Warmly," (too personal for legal practice)
- "Cheers," (informal)

9. Signature Block — Your Professional Identity

Include:

- name
- title
- firm
- phone
- email

This is your digital business card.

10. Email Tone: Neutral, Respectful, Confident

Tone is everything.

Professional tone is:

- calm
- neutral
- respectful

- confident
- concise

Avoid:

- sarcasm
- frustration
- defensiveness
- emotional language

Emails live forever. Write accordingly.

11. Common Email Scenarios (With Templates)

Below are the emails new lawyers send most often — with templates you can adapt.

A. Delivering an Assignment

Subject: Draft Memo on Duty of Care

Hi [Name],

Attached is the draft memorandum you requested. It includes an analysis of the voluntary-undertaking doctrine and its application to our facts. Please let me know if you'd like me to expand any section or conduct additional research.

Best,

[Signature]

B. Asking a Clarifying Question

Subject: Question About Research Scope

Hi [Name],

I'm working on the research assignment regarding the duty of care.

Before I proceed further, I want to confirm whether you'd like me to include out-of-state cases or limit the analysis to New York authority.

Thank you,

[Signature]

C. Updating a Client

Subject: Update on Your Case — Doe v. Metro Co.

Dear Mr. Doe,

I'm writing to update you on the status of your case. We filed the Motion for Summary Judgment on March 10, and Metro Co. has until April 5 to respond. I will notify you as soon as the court schedules the next step. Please feel free to reach out with any questions.

Best,

[Signature]

D. Following Up (Professionally)

Subject: Follow-Up on Assignment

Hi [Name],

I'm following up on the draft motion I sent yesterday. Please let me know if you have any edits or if you'd like me to begin revising.

Best,

[Signature]

E. Emailing Opposing Counsel

Subject: Meet-and-Confer Request — Doe v. Metro Co.

Dear Counsel,

I am writing to request a meet-and-confer regarding the outstanding discovery issues in this matter. Please let me know your availability this week.

Regards,

[Signature]

12. The "Before You Send" Checklist

Before you hit send, ask:

- Is the subject line clear?
- Is the purpose sentence clear?
- Is the tone professional?
- Is the email concise?
- Are there any typos?
- Is the attachment included?
- Is the signature block correct?

This checklist prevents 90% of email mistakes.

13. Email as a Professional Identity

Your emails become:

- your reputation
- your reliability
- your voice
- your brand

Clear emails build trust. Confident emails build credibility.

Professional emails build careers.

CHAPTER SIXTEEN

Building Your Legal Writing Portfolio

How to Curate, Organize, and Present Your Best Legal Work With Confidence and Professionalism

A legal writing portfolio is more than a collection of documents. It is a **professional identity**, a curated showcase of your:

- clarity
- structure
- analysis
- judgment
- professionalism
- growth

This chapter teaches you how to build a portfolio that reflects your strengths, your voice, and your readiness for practice.

1. What a Legal Writing Portfolio Is (and Isn't)

A legal writing portfolio is:

- a curated set of writing samples
- chosen to demonstrate your skills
- organized to highlight your strengths
- polished to professional standards

A legal writing portfolio is **not**:

- a dump of everything you've ever written
- a collection of unedited drafts
- a place for confidential or privileged material

- a place for personal essays or creative writing

Your portfolio is a **professional artifact** — a legal calling card.

2. The Architecture of a Strong Portfolio

A strong portfolio includes:

1. **A polished legal memorandum**
2. **A polished motion or brief**
3. **A client-facing document**
4. **A professional email sample**
5. **Optional: A research summary or case brief**
6. **Optional: A demand letter or negotiation document**
7. **Optional: A writing sample tailored to your specialty**

Each piece should demonstrate:

- structure
- clarity
- analysis
- tone control
- professionalism

Your portfolio should feel like a **cohesive collection**, not a random assortment.

3. Choosing Your Best Work

When selecting pieces, ask:

- Does this show my strongest writing?
- Does this show my ability to analyze?

- Does this show my ability to communicate clearly?
- Does this show my ability to write for different audiences?
- Does this show my growth?

Choose pieces that reflect:

- your voice
- your precision
- your professionalism

Quality matters more than quantity.

4. Editing Your Portfolio Pieces

Every piece must be:

- polished
- proofread
- formatted correctly
- cited accurately
- free of confidential information

Use the editing techniques from Chapter Fourteen:

- structural editing
- clarity editing
- conciseness editing
- technical editing

Your portfolio should feel **court-ready**.

5. Removing Confidential or Privileged Information

Never include:

- client names
- case numbers
- identifying facts
- privileged communications
- internal firm strategy

If you must use real work:

- redact identifying details
- change names
- change dates
- change locations
- change non-essential facts

Or better yet:

- use writing from law school
- use writing from clinics
- use writing from moot court
- use writing created specifically for your portfolio

Your portfolio must be ethical.

6. Writing New Pieces for Your Portfolio

If you don't have strong samples, create them.

You can write:

- a mock memorandum
- a mock motion
- a mock brief

- a mock client letter
- a mock demand letter

Use the templates and annotated samples from Chapter Eleven.

Your portfolio is not a record of your past — it is a **presentation of your potential**.

7. Organizing Your Portfolio

Your portfolio should be:

- clean
- simple
- professional
- easy to navigate

Use this structure:

A. Cover Page

- your name
- your contact information
- a short professional statement

B. Table of Contents

- list each sample
- include short descriptions

C. Writing Samples

Organized by category:

1. **Legal Analysis**
2. **Persuasive Writing**

3. **Client Communication**
4. **Professional Communication**
5. **Optional Specialty Writing**

Each sample should begin with:

- a title
- a one-sentence description
- the purpose of the document
- the audience

This helps the reader understand context.

8. Digital vs. Physical Porfolios

Digital Porfolio

- PDF format
- clean layout
- clickable table of contents
- easy to email
- easy to update

Physical Portfolio

- binder or folder
- printed on quality paper
- tabs for each section
- used for interviews

Most professionals maintain both.

9. Tailoring Your Portfolio to Opportunities

Customize your portfolio for:

- clerkships
- internships
- law firms
- government roles
- compliance roles
- policy roles
- inhouse roles

For example:

Litigation roles

Include motions, briefs, and memos.

Transactional roles

Include contracts, client letters, and negotiation documents.

Compliance roles

Include risk assessments, policy memos, and regulatory summaries.

Your portfolio should speak the language of the job you want.

10. Presenting Your Portfolio With Confidence

When sharing your portfolio:

- introduce it briefly
- highlight your strongest piece
- explain your writing process
- show pride in your work
- be ready to discuss revisions

Your portfolio is a conversation starter — a way to show your growth, your discipline, and your professionalism.

11. Your Portfolio as a Living Document

Your portfolio will evolve as you:

- grow
- write more
- refine your voice
- gain experience

Update it regularly.

Your portfolio is not a snapshot — it is a **story of your development**.

CHAPTER SEVENTEEN

Advanced Persuasive Writing Techniques

How to Influence, Guide, and Move Your Reader With Precision and Power

Persuasive writing is not about emotion. It is not about theatrics. It is not about cleverness.

Persuasive writing is about **guiding the reader's mind** — step by step, fact by fact, rule by rule — until the conclusion feels inevitable.

This chapter teaches you the advanced techniques lawyers use to persuade judges, supervisors, clients, and opposing counsel.

These techniques are subtle, powerful, and rooted in clarity, structure, and human psychology.

1. The Core Principle of Persuasion: Make It Easy to Agree With You

Judges are busy. Supervisors are busy. Clients are overwhelmed.

Your job is to:

- reduce cognitive load
- simplify complexity
- guide the reader
- remove friction
- make agreement feel natural

Persuasion is not force. Persuasion is **ease**.

2. The Architecture of Persuasive Writing

Persuasive writing has three pillars:

A. Structure

A clear, predictable structure builds trust.

B. Clarity

A clear argument is a persuasive argument.

C. Credibility

Credibility is the currency of persuasion.

If the reader trusts you, they will follow you.

3. The Psychology of Persuasion in Legal Writing

Persuasive writing uses:

- priming
- framing
- emphasis
- contrast
- narrative logic
- cognitive ease

These are not tricks. These are tools.

Let's break them down.

4. Priming: Setting the Reader's Expectations

Priming means preparing the reader's mind before presenting the argument.

Example:

"Because the defendant voluntarily undertook responsibility for the plaintiff's safety, the court should find that a duty existed."

This primes the reader to expect:

- responsibility
- reliance
- duty

Priming creates a mental frame that makes your conclusion feel natural.

5. Framing: Choosing the Lens Through Which the Reader Sees the Facts

Facts do not speak for themselves. You choose the frame.

Neutral Frame:

"The defendant inspected the scaffolding."

Persuasive Frame:

"The defendant personally inspected the scaffolding and assured the plaintiff it was safe."

Same fact. Different frame. Different impact.

6. The Power of the First Sentence in Every Section

The first sentence of:

- your introduction
- your argument
- your paragraphs
- your headings

…sets the tone and direction.

A strong first sentence:

- states the conclusion
- frames the issue

- guides the reader

Example:

"Defendant owed a duty of care because he voluntarily undertook responsibility for Plaintiff's safety."

This is persuasion through clarity.

7. Headings as Persuasion

Headings are not labels. Headings are **arguments**.

Weak Heading:

"Duty of Care"

Strong Heading:

"Defendant Owed a Duty of Care Under the Voluntary-Undertaking Doctrine."

Headings should:

- be complete sentences
- state legal conclusions
- guide the reader

Headings are the skeleton of persuasion.

8. The CREAC Advantage: Why Structure Persuades

CREAC persuades because it:

- reduces cognitive load
- creates predictability
- builds momentum
- reinforces conclusions

Judges trust CREAC because it feels orderly and logical.

9. The Strategic Use of Facts

Facts persuade when they are:

- concrete
- specific
- relevant
- placed strategically

Technique: The "Golden Fact"

Identify the one fact that makes your case strongest.

Place it:

- in the introduction
- in the first paragraph of the argument
- in the application section

Repetition (used sparingly) reinforces importance.

10. Using Case Law Persuasively

Case law persuades when you:

- choose the right cases
- explain the rule clearly
- highlight similarities
- distinguish differences
- use parentheticals strategically

Persuasive Parenthetical:

(holding that a duty arises when a defendant's assurances create foreseeable reliance)

Parentheticals are mini-arguments.

11. The Power of Contrast

Contrast strengthens your argument by showing:

- why your case fits the rule
- why the opposing case does not
- why your interpretation is more logical

Example:

"Unlike the defendant in Smith, who provided no assurances, Defendant here personally inspected the scaffolding and assured Plaintiff it was safe."

Contrast clarifies.

12. Strategic Conciseness

Conciseness is persuasive because:

- it respects the reader's time
- it reduces cognitive load
- it highlights key points
- it eliminates noise

Cut ruthlessly. Clarity is persuasion.

13. Transitions as Persuasive Glue

Transitions guide the reader through your reasoning.

Use:

- “Therefore…”
- “Because…”
- “In contrast…”
- “Similarly…”
- “As a result…”

Transitions create flow. Flow creates persuasion.

14. The Persuasive Introduction

A persuasive introduction:

- states the conclusion
- states the reason
- previews the structure
- frames the issue

Example:

“The court should grant summary judgment because Defendant voluntarily undertook responsibility for Plaintiff's safety and breached that duty. The undisputed facts show that Defendant inspected the scaffolding, assured Plaintiff it was safe, and failed to secure it.”

Short. Clear. Persuasive.

15. The Persuasive Conclusion

A persuasive conclusion:

- restates the conclusion

- reinforces the logic
- ends with confidence

Example:

"For these reasons, the court should grant summary judgment in Plaintiff's favor."

Simple. Direct. Powerful.

16. Persuasion With Humanity (The Law in Pieces Signature)

Your writing is persuasive because it is:

- clear
- warm
- human
- narrative
- architectural

You do not manipulate. You illuminate.

You do not overwhelm. You guide.

You do not pressure. You persuade through clarity, dignity, and structure.

This is the Law in Pieces way.

CHAPTER EIGHTEEN

Writing for Clients, Courts, and Colleagues

How to Adapt Your Voice, Tone, and Structure to Every Audience You Serve

Legal writing is not one voice. It is many voices — each shaped by the audience, the purpose, and the professional relationship.

A judge needs clarity and structure. A client needs reassurance and plain language. A supervising attorney needs accuracy and judgment. Opposing counsel needs professionalism and precision.

This chapter teaches you how to shift your voice with intention, confidence, and mastery.

1. Why Audience Matters More Than Anything Else

The same facts can be written:

- formally for a court
- plainly for a client
- strategically for opposing counsel
- concisely for a colleague

Your audience determines:

- tone
- structure
- vocabulary
- level of detail
- emotional temperature
- formality

Audience is the architect of your writing.

2. Writing for Courts

Tone: Formal, neutral, structured, authoritative

Courts want:

- clarity
- structure
- neutrality
- accuracy
- professionalism

They do **not** want:

- emotion
- exaggeration
- rhetorical flourishes
- personal attacks
- unnecessary detail

The Court Voice

- precise
- restrained
- respectful
- logical
- citation-driven

Court Writing Priorities

1. **Structure** (CREAC, headings, roadmap)
2. **Clarity** (short sentences, strong verbs)
3. **Authority** (cases, statutes, rules)
4. **Neutrality** (no emotional language)
5. **Professionalism** (clean formatting, correct citations)

Example (Court Voice)

"Defendant owed a duty of care because he voluntarily undertook responsibility for Plaintiff's safety. Courts impose such a duty when a defendant's assurances create foreseeable reliance."

3. Writing for Clients

Tone: Warm, clear, plain, reassuring

Clients want:

- clarity
- plain English
- reassurance
- next steps
- transparency

They do **not** want:

- legal jargon
- citations
- dense paragraphs
- uncertainty without explanation

The Client Voice

- human
- calm
- clear
- supportive
- plain language

Client Writing Priorities

1. **Explain the situation**
2. **Explain what it means**
3. **Explain next steps**
4. **Explain what the client must do**
5. **Reassure without overpromising**

Example (Client Voice)

"We filed your motion on March 10. The other side has until April 5 to respond. After that, the court may schedule a hearing or decide the motion based on the written documents. You do not need to take any action right now."

4. Writing for Supervising Attorneys

Tone: Clear, concise, accurate, analytical

Supervising attorneys want:

- accuracy
- judgment
- clarity
- efficiency

- reliability

They do **not** want:

- long explanations
- emotional language
- uncertainty without options
- buried conclusions

The Supervisor Voice

- concise
- analytical
- neutral
- organized
- solution-oriented

Supervisor Writing Priorities

1. **Answer the question**
2. **Explain the rule**
3. **Apply the rule**
4. **Identify open issues**
5. **Recommend next steps**

Example (Supervisor Voice)

"The voluntary-undertaking doctrine applies because Defendant provided assurances that Plaintiff relied on. Two cases support this conclusion; one is distinguishable. I recommend citing Johnson as the primary authority."

5. Writing for Opposing Counsel

Tone: Professional, firm, respectful, precise

Opposing counsel wants:

- clarity
- professionalism
- boundaries
- accuracy

They do **not** want:

- hostility
- sarcasm
- threats
- emotional language

The Opposing Counsel Voice

- firm
- respectful
- direct
- precise
- strategic

Opposing Counsel Writing Priorities

1. **State the issue**
2. **State your position**
3. **State what you need**
4. **State the deadline**
5. **Remain professional**

Example (Opposing Counsel Voice)

"We request that you produce the outstanding documents by April 12. If we do not receive them by that date, we will seek court intervention."

6. Writing for Colleagues

Tone: Efficient, clear, collaborative

Colleagues want:

- clarity
- efficiency
- context
- next steps

They do **not** want:

- long emails
- unnecessary detail
- emotional tone

The Colleague Voice

- concise
- friendly
- clear
- collaborative

Example (Colleague Voice)

"Here are the three cases we discussed. The second one is the strongest for our argument. Let me know if you want me to draft the summary."

7. How to Shift Your Voice Without Losing Yourself

Your voice remains:

- clear
- warm
- human
- structured

But you adjust:

- formality
- vocabulary
- detail
- tone

Think of it like adjusting lighting in a room — the structure stays the same, but the atmosphere changes.

8. Side-by-Side Examples (Same Facts, Different Audiences)

Court Version

"Defendant owed a duty of care because he voluntarily undertook responsibility for Plaintiff's safety."

Client Version

"The company became responsible for your safety when their supervisor told you the scaffolding was secure."

Supervisor Version

"The voluntary-undertaking doctrine applies because Defendant provided assurances that created reliance."

Opposing Counsel Version

"Your client assumed responsibility for Plaintiff's safety when he assured him the scaffolding was secure."

Colleague Version

"The duty issue is strong — the supervisor's assurance triggers the voluntary-undertaking doctrine."

Same fact. Different voice. Different purpose.

9. The Law in Pieces Philosophy of Audience-Driven Writing

- clarity is kindness
- structure is respect
- tone is strategy
- humanity is strength

CHAPTER NINETEEN

The Emotional Side of Legal Writing — Confidence, Shame, and Growth

Why Legal Writing Hurts, How It Heals, and How to Build a Voice That Believes in Itself

Legal writing is not just a skill. It is an emotional experience.

Every sentence carries:

- your confidence
- your fear
- your past
- your training
- your wounds
- your resilience

1. Why Legal Writing Feels Personal

Legal writing feels personal because:

- it is public
- it is judged
- it is graded
- it is edited
- it is compared
- it is tied to identity
- it is tied to belonging

When someone critiques your writing, it can feel like they are critiquing you.

But writing is not identity. Writing is a skill — one that grows, evolves, and strengthens with practice.

2. Shame: The Silent Barrier to Growth

Shame is the most common — and least discussed — obstacle in legal writing.

Shame sounds like:

- "I'm not good enough."
- "Everyone else understands this except me."
- "I'm behind."
- "I'm slow."
- "I'm not smart enough."
- "I don't belong here."

Shame is not a sign of weakness. Shame is a sign that you care.

But shame blocks learning. Shame shuts down curiosity. Shame makes you afraid to ask questions. Shame makes you hide.

This chapter is your antidote.

3. Confidence: The Skill You Build, Not the Trait You Have

Confidence is not a personality trait. Confidence is a **practice**.

Confidence grows when you:

- understand structure
- understand expectations
- understand your audience
- understand your purpose
- understand your tools

Confidence is clarity. Confidence is repetition. Confidence is mastery built slowly, piece by piece.

4. The Myth of the "Natural Writer"

There is no such thing as a natural legal writer.

Legal writing is:

- learned
- practiced
- refined
- edited
- built

If legal writing feels hard, it's because it *is* hard — not because you're failing.

5. The Emotional Architecture of Legal Writing

Legal writing requires:

A. Vulnerability

You put your thinking on the page.

B. Courage

You risk being wrong.

C. Humility

You accept edits.

D. Resilience

You revise again.

E. Curiosity

You ask questions.

F. Self-trust

You believe you can improve.

These are emotional skills, not technical ones.

6. The Role of Feedback: How to Receive It Without Losing Yourself

Feedback is not a verdict. Feedback is a tool.

But many students experience feedback as:

- rejection
- judgment
- failure
- exposure

Here is the truth:

Feedback is not about you. Feedback is about the document.

You are not your draft. You are the writer who will revise it.

7. How to Build Emotional Resilience in Legal Writing

1. Separate identity from performance

You are not your draft.

2. Expect edits

Edits are normal, constant, and universal.

3. Normalize confusion

Confusion is the beginning of clarity.

4. Ask questions early

Questions show professionalism, not weakness.

5. Celebrate progress, not perfection

Perfection is not the goal. Clarity is.

6. Build rituals that support your writing

- a clean workspace
- a consistent process
- a checklist
- a template
- a deep breath before you begin

Rituals reduce anxiety.

8. Growth: The Quiet, Powerful Transformation

Growth in legal writing is:

- incremental
- invisible at first
- cumulative
- inevitable with practice

Growth looks like:

- clearer sentences
- stronger headings
- better structure
- faster drafting
- calmer editing
- more confidence

Growth is not loud. Growth is steady.

9. The Law in Pieces Promise: You Belong Here

You belong in the law. Your voice belongs in the law. Your story belongs in the law. Your writing belongs in the law.

You are not behind. You are not late. You are not alone.

You are building something — piece by piece — that will carry you through your career.

10. I want you to know that you are capable; you are more than enough. Believe in yourself.

You are not the red ink on your first memo. You are not the silence you kept in class. You are not the fear you felt when you opened your first assignment. You are the writer who kept going. You are the writer who is learning. You are the writer who is growing. You are the writer who is building a voice that will change things.

You are not behind. You are becoming.

ABOUT THE AUTHOR

A.G. Seymour is a visionary law tutor, compliance specialist, and author of more than twenty-four books. With an LL.M. from the University of Maryland Francis King Carey School of Law, an LL.B. (Hons.), from the University of London, and certification as a Risk & Compliance Management Professional (CRCMP), she brings a rare combination of academic rigor, regulatory insight, and creative storytelling to the study of law.

Her Law in Pieces series reimagines legal education through anatomically structured case dissections, and emotionally resonant pedagogy designed to spark epiphany. Anjanette G. Seymour believes that every student deserves to feel seen, capable, and at home in the law — and she writes with that mission at heart.

Beyond the page, she is a designer, mentor, and advocate for accessible legal learning, weaving art, narrative, and doctrine into a unified legacy of empowerment.

www.ingramcontent.com/pod-product-compliance
Lightning Source LLC
LaVergne TN
LVHW022221200926
848481LV00006B/2058
* 9 7 9 8 9 9 5 8 9 2 3 5 9 *